University of Cincinnati Classical Studies

III

Urbanitas: ANCIENT SOPHISTICATION AND REFINEMENT

Urbanitas

ANCIENT SOPHISTICATION
AND REFINEMENT

By Edwin S. Ramage

PUBLISHED BY THE UNIVERSITY OF OKLAHOMA PRESS
FOR THE UNIVERSITY OF CINCINNATI

Library of Congress Cataloging in Publication Data

Ramage, Edwin S.   1929–
  Urbanitas.
  Bibliography: p.
  1. Rome—Social life and customs. 2. Greece—Social life and customs.
I. Title.
DE71.R35   309.1'38   72–9257
ISBN 0–8061–1063–5

ACKNOWLEDGMENT

The author wishes to thank the Louise Taft Semple Classics Fund of the University of Cincinnati for making publication of this study possible.

To My Wife, Sue

PREFACE

This study of Roman urbanity and sophistication was begun as a doctoral dissertation at the University of Cincinnati in 1957. In the years that have followed much has been added and much has been modified.

Many people have helped, but my special thanks must go to Professor Carl R. Trahman of the University of Cincinnati, who not only spent much time and effort on the dissertation, but put in many hours reading drafts of the present manuscript. Whatever is useful I must share with him; the mistakes and misinterpretations are mine alone.

Lynne L. Merritt, Jr., Vice-President and Dean for Research and Advanced Studies at Indiana University, and others in his office have generously provided financial support for basic research and preparation of the manuscript.

Research has also been facilitated by Professor W. Ehlers and the staff of the *Thesaurus Linguae Latinae*, who willingly supplied complete runs on *scurra* and its cognates along with detailed supplements to the standard indices for *urbanus-urbanitas, rusticus-rusticitas*, and *peregrinus-peregrinitas*.

Finally, I must express my appreciation to the Department of Classics and the Louise Taft Semple Classics Fund of the University of Cincinnati for making publication possible.

The sad news of Professor Donald W. Bradeen's sudden death came when these pages were in the last stages of proof. And so it was with a profound sense of loss that I turned to the final corrections. We who were his students have lost a fine teacher, a distinguished scholar, a loyal mentor, and a close friend.

EDWIN S. RAMAGE

Bloomington, Indiana
May 15, 1973

CONTENTS

Urbanitas: ANCIENT SOPHISTICATION AND REFINEMENT

INTRODUCTION

Though sophistication is an abstract concept that is difficult to define, most people nowadays have some idea of what it involves. Refinement, sophistication, or urbanity—whatever we choose to call it—might be best described as the outward manifestation of an inner culture acquired from residing in or at least having contact with an urban center. The connection with the city need not be as close today as it was earlier, since improved communication has done much to spread urban influence to the smaller towns and countryside. It is still from the society of the large city, however, that standards of refinement emanate.

The gentleman who comes from this environment leads a life that is governed by a sense of decorum and propriety which manifests itself in everything he does and says. He wears the latest fashions discreetly and with aplomb, and his manners are both modern and impeccable. The way he talks is extremely important, for it is perhaps the most significant way he has of showing his sense of good taste and good manners. As he speaks, the gentleman couches what he has to say in the proper language, bringing into play a ready, subtle wit and overlaying it all with a cultured, cultivated accent. There is extreme pressure on him to maintain these standards, though in many quarters nowadays such a tendency to conform, if it is not rejected outright, is at least viewed with suspicion.

But the gentleman is not as closely typed by his habits and out-

3

look as might be expected, for the various traits appear to different degrees and in varying combinations from one person to the other, so that each urbane man remains an individual and the complete gentleman remains an ideal. He retains his individuality in yet another way, for he takes his refinement, particularly in its details, from the city in which he lives, and his city is quite unlike all others. Thus a man of Rome, while he will have much in common with his counterpart in Paris or London, will be different from both of them, and they in turn will differ from one another.

A person who carefully cultivates his own urbanity also exhibits clearly discernible attitudes to the world around him. Perhaps the most common is a feeling of condescension or even intolerance toward those who do not reach his standards. The attitude of the town-dweller to the rustic, for example, which has existed since man first began to surround himself with walls, is familiar to everyone.

By now the names of certain cities have become synonymous with such feelings and outlook. A mere mention of Bath, for example, conjures up a picture of tasteful manners and cultivated outlook which in stereotype lend themselves to easy satire under the pen of a writer like Jane Austen or Charles Dickens. Lewis Mumford has described this center as "the most consistently urbane of English cities, which in its best days boasted the population of a country town and cultivated the polite airs of a metropolis."[1] The "polite airs" are still there for anyone who cares to visit.

Contemporary society throughout the world is well laced with such sentiments. The feeling that the New Yorker has for the average person from the midwestern United States, for instance, springs straight from a conviction that the touchstone of American urbanity enjoys a permanent resting place in downtown Manhattan. The Parisian, too, is quick to express criticism of people not only from other parts of his own country, but also from the rest of the world, especially when food, clothing, and language come up for discussion. The contemporary Roman's prejudices against the man from Naples may go deeper than matters of taste and manners, but these certainly play their part, as any perceptive traveler can see for himself.

In ancient Rome the sophisticated Roman gentleman, the *urbanus homo*, was equally recognizable. His refinement was called *urbanitas*, and, though the Romans may not have successfully defined the phenomenon, they were fully aware of the important influence that it had on their thought, habits, and actions. It quite literally governed the lives of men like Ovid and Petronius and was so important a constituent of Cicero's thinking that the orator imagined its disappearance as heralding the downfall of the Republic. At the other extreme *urbanitas* was used to describe the special Roman wit for which the orator and other educated Romans were striving and could even be applied to the smart, sophisticated cap in an epigram.

The attitudes to which this feeling gave rise are also very much in evidence. It is at least partly an awareness of this sophistication that makes Lucilius at one time laugh at a boor from the country and at another take issue with well-bred Romans for exhibiting a rustic accent or for adopting Greek culture too willingly. Again, Cicero maintains reservations about extra-Roman orators because they do not have the urban and urbane accent. Ovid's attachment to the city and its sophisticated life made his exile on the Black Sea a living hell.

By now it is perhaps clear why Roman urbanity deserves study, but where do we begin and how do we proceed with such an investigation? Because *urbanitas* is an abstract concept and because the evidence is for the most part scattered as brief and incidental references through many authors, further complexity must be avoided. The arrangement that suggests itself as most obvious is the chronological. The Greek background must also be taken into account because of the influence that Classical Greece had on Roman attitudes, especially in Republican times. We shall begin with the earliest traces, then, but to find a lower limit is not easy, for *urbanitas* never really disappeared. The choice of Pliny the Younger to terminate the study is rather arbitrary, although it may be proposed as a defense that Rome of the classical era is the subject of the investigation, and this writer comes roughly at the end of this period. At the same time, Pliny is a well-documented *urbanus homo* and so provides a suitably positive note on which to end.

Finally, a word of caution is in order. Because the organization is chronological, evolutional elements may be expected to appear. But theories of evolution and development must be controlled. In his book *The Ancient Romances*, Perry has made the important point that literary theory is too tightly bound to ideas of constant, consistent development.[2] What he says here applies rather well to manners, taste, and the like, for in this case it is equally dangerous to strait-jacket the evidence to produce a tightly compartmentalized scheme.

Some of those who have examined *urbanitas* in one or more of its manifestations, failing to recognize that sophistication or refinement is an essence, an aura, a subtle abstraction that makes itself felt in impressions, feelings, and attitudes, have treated it as a specimen that can be slipped under a microscope. A glance at the contemporary situation shows not only how wrong it is, but also how dangerous it is to use methods that imply logical development, for norms of behavior, if they may still be called that, exist today that were not even conceived of five, ten, twenty, or fifty years ago. In fact, criteria sometimes seem to change from day to day. The reasons for this are perfectly obvious: attitudes and outlook are for the most part the result of an interworking of a complex of political, economic, and social circumstances which are themselves constantly changing at different rates. Perhaps, then, it is better not to use words like "evolution" and "development" at all, but rather to speak of "change" which may be gradual or sudden, subtle or violent, forward or backward.

In the case of Roman urbanity it is logical to expect that in the early centuries as the city took form the Romans acquired a basic culture by a process that may be described as gradual. But the introduction of literature must have given sudden impetus to such tendencies, so that it is wrong to assume that the urbanity of Scipionic times evolved smoothly into that of the Ciceronian period, and that the sophisticated behavior and outlook of late Republican times was shaped slowly but surely into an Augustan refinement. Theory is not enough; proof must be found, or the question must be left open. And so in the account which follows, reference will be made to evolutional elements and characteristics where they can be identified, but a careful and conscious effort will be made not to imprint patterns where none exist.

CHAPTER I

GREEK URBANITY IN
THE CLASSICAL PERIOD
AND AFTER

Refinement and the attitudes which accompany it are mentioned frequently in extant Greek literature, and the Roman, whether like Scipio he was an ardent admirer of the urbane Xenophon or whether like Terence or Cicero he was bringing the civilized philosophy of a Menander or a Panaetius into Latin, could not miss such pronouncements. Some description of Greek urbanity is necessary, then, though it is clearly impossible to carry out a detailed survey. A glance at the sources shows, however, that there are four accounts which when taken together give a fair idea of what the sophisticated Greek was like and how he thought.

First, there is Pericles as he is portrayed by Thucydides (2.35–46) giving the famous funeral oration over the Athenians who had fallen in the first year of the Peloponnesian War. Reinforcing this fifth century picture of urbanity is the characterization of a sophisticated Socrates that Plato presents in his Dialogues. A little less than a century later Menander produced his *Dyscolus* in which urban society played a leading part as the playwright studied the problems that resulted from a confrontation between a thoroughgoing urbanity and a complete rusticity. Finally, there are the Greek romances where an ideal Hellenistic refinement is part of the generally romantic atmosphere.

Though the speech that Pericles gave in 430 B.C. is much more than simply a show of sophistication and refinement, it is impossible to miss such overtones. The speaker stresses throughout an

Athenian exclusiveness that is especially apparent in matters of government where the people of Athens have not only adopted little or nothing from others but have also provided a pattern for their contemporaries in other states to follow. Pericles also makes much of the fact that in both public and private affairs the man of Athens maintains a strict sense of decorum and restraint. He is careful, for example, not to give offense to anyone and avoids extravagance or softness when he expresses his appreciation of truth and beauty. This sense of decorum enables him to blend the correct amount of daring with careful reflection and so escape the ignorance and hesitation which often characterize the decisions of others. In other words, he avoids any boorishness and rusticity in his approach to life. Finally, there is a strong sense of generosity that makes itself felt in the Athenian's desire to confer honors rather than receive them. An important contributing factor in all of this is a life which provides the right education and ample opportunity for pleasant relaxation in an environment that is aesthetically satisfying.

It should be noticed that as he speaks Pericles scrupulously observes the politeness and restraint with which he characterizes his fellow citizens, for nowhere does he make any extravagant claims and he constantly blends daring and careful reflection to the degree which he advocates. The speaker reveals himself, then, as an ideal product of the education, leisure, and beauty that the city has to offer.[1] But what he says must be put in the proper perspective, for the picture of the contemporary situation that Pericles presents is far more ideal than the true state of affairs. It must also be kept in mind that Pericles is not talking to the whole populace, for the rustic element, among others, when they heard such sentiments expressed so eloquently could have had no more than a vague idea of what was being said. This was more than likely the kind of thing that Dicaeopolis in Aristophanes' play, the *Acharnians*, and Hermes in his *Peace* are complaining about when they lash out at clever speakers in the city.[2]

The feelings expressed by Pericles in the funeral oration had been arising for some time, for after the wars with Persia the image of Athens as a social and economic center had grown very rapidly. By the time of the Peloponnesian War she had become "the city" as opposed to the countryside, other Greek centers, and even the Piraeus,[3] so that what was located in Athens or what was happening there was designated ἀστικόν, [4] the city's refinement was embraced by the adjective ἀστεῖον, and the Athenian who exhibited this urbanity was an ἀστεῖος ἀνήρ or an urbane man.

A search for a sophisticated Athenian of the late fifth and early fourth centuries B.C. leads straight to the Dialogues of Plato, for here Socrates has taken on most of the characteristics of the gentleman of the time. Plato has him reveal his urbanity in the way he thinks and speaks; restraint, tact, and consideration are his bywords.[5] Socrates is extremely careful at all times not to press his ideas on his hearers but phrases what he has to say in as tactful a manner as possible. He offers contradiction, for example, by softening his statement with a "perhaps," "I should venture to say," or "it seems to me"; if he must bring censure, he does so discreetly, gradually, and gently after establishing rapport. Again, he may graciously deny a wish or decline an invitation by prefacing his refusal with a friendly remark and then carefully choosing his words.

Socrates' side of an extended discussion in the Dialogues is usually laced with indulgence, for it is his practice to draw conversation from his partner and not to make an issue of getting his own ideas expressed. When he does state his thoughts, he applies a restraint and logic to what he is saying, and at the same time is careful to leave the impression that he is open to correction. He also avoids too forthright an approach that could easily develop into a boorish dogmatism by expressing his views as a fear or by using a question.

To reinforce the illusion that every conversation is a two-sided partnership and to further strengthen the impression of modesty and restraint that he wishes to leave, Plato's Socrates tends to avoid the limiting pronoun "I" and to substitute for it the less personal plural form. The wit that the philosopher exhibits is another important manifestation of his refinement, for it is careful and restrained and is brought into play only at the appropriate time.[6] Part of this is the Socratic irony which with its subtle and clever innuendo is meant not only to reveal the speaker's urbanity but also to appeal to the sophisticated palates of Plato's readers. It is worth noting in passing that the Socrates of the Dialogues is essentially a reflection of Plato's urbanity, and so it is dangerous to draw precise conclusions about the real man from the picture presented here.

Though the characterization that Plato presents is fairly complete, it may be supplemented in at least one important respect from evidence that lies outside the Dialogues. A fragment of an unidentified play of Aristophanes[7] suggests that there was an urban way of speaking that had none of the weaknesses and affectations of hypersophistication and at the same time avoided the unpolished idiom and rough accent of the rustic. It is almost impossible to be more precise about the characteristics of urbane speech, but from what Isocrates and Cicero say, it is clear that an urbane Athenian like Thucydides' Pericles or Plato's Socrates was careful to cultivate a tone of voice and a precise pronunciation that would lend an air of smoothness and sweetness to his utterance.[8]

While Thucydides and Plato present the refined Athenian in an urban environment, Menander in the Dyscolus has moved him into a rustic context.[9] Sostratus, a product of the wealth and leisure of the city, has found his way to rough and rocky Phyle, bringing with him his mother, father, family servants, and even a hired cook, all of whom contribute to the contrast which the playwright wishes to describe and analyze. Sostratus is drawn by Menander as a young man of almost perfect culture and his urbanity is kept before the audience throughout the play.

Perhaps the clearest insight into the makeup and workings of his sophistication is provided at his first encounter with the rustic Gorgias (269–319), where, in spite of the sudden, savage, and unwarranted attack by someone he does not even know, the young gentleman calmly bides his time, asks for permission to speak, and then states his position with precision and restraint. It takes a lot to make Sostratus lose his veneer of urbanity. But his blind love for Cnemon's daughter presents a serious strain, for he is, after all, only human. The struggle that takes place within him may be seen clearly in his first encounter with her (199–214), during which he barely manages to maintain his aplomb. His response at this point represents a kind of emotional compromise. While it is the reaction of a lover to rush after the water, it is also the response of a gentleman toward a lady in distress. His actions at the well later in the play (666–90) show the same emotional conflict even more clearly, for he once again lets himself slip for a moment when he is tempted to take her in his arms to comfort her. But Sostratus persists in maintaining his poise against the overwhelming urge, and it is soon evident that his sense of discretion has asserted itself at perhaps the most crucial stage in his relationship with the girl.

But there is also in Sostratus a certain naïveté and impetuousness coming from his urban upbringing that causes him to make mistakes simply because he is remarkably out of place in the country. He believes that a Chaereas or a Pyrrhias can plead his case for him, but it soon becomes apparent that methods which are successful in the city will not work here. His rush to Cnemon's door to speak for himself (148–78, 266f.) and his suggestion of a banquet to cement his friendship with Gorgias (558–62, 611–19) arise partly from his state of mind, but they also represent naïve and not very well considered attempts to deal with rustic people in urban ways. At the same time, it is important to realize that Sostratus' confidence in his ability to solve these problems stems from the fact that he is actually a successful man of action when he is in his own environment. Because he knows exactly how to handle his father, for instance, he succeeds in getting permission not for one marriage but for two.

Although Sostratus is the most important urbanite in the play, the others cannot be ignored. Callippides and his wife, Getas, and Sicon may be personalities commonly found in New Comedy, but in this case their importance lies primarily in the fact that they represent various aspects of life in town. By injecting a hyper-urbanity or a superrefinement into Callippides, the indulgent father, Menander shows what shallowness extreme wealth and leisure can produce. His wife seems to be similarly innocuous and emptyheaded, especially in matters of religion.

While Getas and Sicon reveal no refinement at all, they are as much products of the urban environment as the others are. Getas displays a cleverness that makes him the only city-dweller who can cope with the dyscolus, for not only does he masterfully restrain himself under Cnemon's attack, but he also cleverly parries him with a wit which is missing even in Sostratus (466–80). Sicon, the cook, by contrast is a cowardly, fawning, officious, self-important, egocentric fool who is a creation of the market place and the wealth that is to be found there.[10]

The point was made earlier that an awareness of urbanity could be expected to produce a certain disdain for those who did not exhibit such sophistication. The rejection of the rustic by the urbanite lies behind many of the events and comments of the *Dyscolus*.[11] Callippides' reservations about the marriages and Getas' and Sicon's insults directed at the dyscolus stem, at least in part, from the feeling that the countryman is not as sophisticated as the city-dweller. This attitude had been explored almost a century earlier by Aristophanes who was constantly reminding his readers of the dichotomous nature of Athenian society and the problems it was causing. From the point of view of a sophisticated Socrates in the *Clouds*, for instance, a rustic who does not comprehend what is being taught is a stupid barbarian deserving nothing better than a whipping, or else he is an uncouth boor and a dull-witted country clown who cannot be taught.[12] Elsewhere in Aristophanes' plays rustics are described as being fair game for city merchants and clever orators both of whom dupe them every chance they get.[13] Though the people that feel this way are not all urban gentlemen, the attitude arises from a general awareness that life in the city is more sophisticated than that of the rustics who live outside the walls.

Though written in Roman times, the Greek romances provide an interesting picture of urbanity as it must have existed in Hellenistic times. The society of the novel is essentially a crystallized Hellenistic bourgeoisie, that is, a landed gentry which lives in the city and leaves its land in the hands of tenant farmers and overseers. Dionysius in Chariton's *Chaereas and Callirhoe* and Dionysophanes in Longus' *Daphnis and Chloe* are good examples of such wealthy landowners. Dionysius, who has been well educated in his youth, enjoys a position at Miletus that makes him a good friend even of the Great King (1.12.6). Signs of his affluence include a large home in the city where he spends most of his time and an extensive and prosperous estate with a comfortable, well-equipped country villa (1.13). Dionysius is so thoroughly committed to an urban existence that he goes out to his farm only at certain times of the year. Dionysophanes is another wealthy city-dweller who looks in on his holdings only at vintage time (4.1).

The urbanity which characterizes the members of this society appears everywhere in these novels, for nearly every one is the story of a member or members of a cultured Greek minority being buffeted about by less desirable and less civilized elements in contemporary society. Callirhoe shows the effect that this conflict can have as she prepares to leave her world for the world of the Great King (5.1.5ff.). She misses her native Greek language and laments that she can no longer see the friendly Mediterranean, for, even though Ionia is a foreign land, it is at least Greek, whereas she must now leave for a completely barbarian existence.

But in spite of the fact that polite society is at center stage most of the time, there is far less by way of detailed information about matters of sophistication than might be expected. The reason for this is simply that the society of Greek Romance has become so thoroughly conventionalized that few individuals exist. There are only types that exhibit formalized reactions and habits, so that the world of a Socrates or a Sostratus in which responses are largely individual and spontaneous has been replaced by an impersonal atmosphere where behavior is controlled by a strict protocol that is never explained.

The gentleman turns up in many guises in the novel. The sophisticated father, who is often a shadowy character, is usually wealthy, easy-going, and indulgent. He may be a political and social leader as Chaereas' father, or his position may be left to the reader's imagination as is the case with Dionysophanes in *Daphnis and Chloe*. The young hero and heroine provide more satisfactory evidence of urbanity, however, inasmuch as they usually have leading parts to play in the action. The young man is typically handsome and comes from a leading family, while the young lady is beautiful and is similarly wellborn. They are therefore symbols of a cultured society, and the tie that binds them is another such symbol, for love is the product of the wealth and leisure of urban life.

Although the sophisticated young lady does not appear often in Greek literature before this time, she has an important role in Romance. Because her breeding is the result of wealth, position, and associations that characterize life in the city, she is quick to stress her pedigree, as Chariclea does in the *Aethiopica* (1.22.2) and Leucippe in Achilles Tatius' *Clitophon and Leucippe* (6.16.6). As Longus points out, her beauty, too, is a characteristic of the city (1.7), so that it comes as no surprise to find out that the fairness of Chariton's Callirhoe is in striking contrast to the plainness of the women on Dionysius' farm (2.1.5).

Just as her beauty sets the heroine off physically from those who surround her, so her good breeding produces a sort of super-modesty which shows itself best in her amorous relations with her hero, particularly in her refusal to have anything to do with other would-be lovers. But this modesty influences the young lady's actions in other ways. A girl like Callirhoe, for example, simply cannot know the habits of slaves (2.10.7) and in her relations with this lower class must maintain a certain aloofness and restraint (6.5.8). Her refinement, then, consists of a sense of propriety that can be expected to assert itself on all occasions.

The urbane young hero is more clearly characterized in these novels, partly because more of the action centers around him, but also because the gentleman has long been portrayed in literature and is more clearly typed. His habits are not radically different from those of his predecessors. The wealthy young men of Methymna who appear hunting, fishing, and fowling in *Daphnis and Chloe* (2.12) and the urbane Astylus who comes from the city to hunt (4.11) call to mind Sostratus as he appears on a similar expedition at the beginning of the *Dyscolus.*

Achilles Tatius provides an interesting picture of how such a gallant is made as he shows the metamorphosis of Callisthenes. This young man is completely out of control when he first appears, never curbing his temper and living a generally loose, extrava-gant, unscrupulous life (2.13). Under the influence of a sincere and honest love, however, he becomes a slave to Calligone and shows his devotion by treating her with respect at all times and even arranging an honorable marriage. In the end he turns out to be an all-round gentleman, very polite, very reasonable, and thoroughly discreet. His urbanity reveals itself not only in a respect-ful generosity, but also in his careful attention to amenities like rising for an elder and speaking first when another approaches (8.17). And yet, even though Callisthenes now displays a subtle combination of restraint, modesty, good manners, and unselfish-ness, the debilitating effect of the transformation is perfectly obvious. He takes his place in the ranks of the bland and relatively colorless heroes of Greek Romance who are for the most part victims of their own urbanity.

To a large extent it is the authors and their concept of characterization that make their heroes this way, but at the same time it is important to realize that these characters are in a direct line from Menander's Sostratus who, as has already been noticed, is completely ineffectual when he tries to act under circumstances that are much removed from the ideal. These young men have carried this tendency to an extreme that leaves them generally incapable of acting in any situation involving trial and tribulation. But Sostratus, though in many ways he is a shallow individual, remains a real, breathing, living person throughout the *Dyscolus*, while crystallization, stylization, and exaggeration have made the gentleman of the novel stiff, unreal, and far less than human.

There is another point of comparison that can be made between Sostratus and Chariton's Chaereas. Menander's hero when out of his element is helpless, while in the city he is a successful man of action. For much of Chariton's novel Chaereas is similarly impotent, mainly because he is in an alien environment without resources of any kind. But he shows that he can act quickly and effectively under the proper stimulation, for when the Egyptians are searching for ways to take Tyre from the Persians and their allies, Chaereas quickly volunteers for the difficult task (7.3f.) and suddenly becomes the cool, calm, methodical general inspiring his band of Greeks on to victory. The reason for the sudden change, though it is not particularly well motivated from the literary point of view, is simply that Chaereas as the son of the officer who is second in command at Syracuse has found a situation that he understands and can control.

A final parallel that may be drawn between the gentleman of New Comedy and his counterpart in the novel lies in the philanthropia or sense of humanity which is very much a part of both. Chariton makes certain that the reader does not miss it in the case

17

of Dionysius, for he not only has this gentleman assert that he is well known for his piety and his philanthropia (2.5.4), but also makes Callirhoe call him "a Greek . . . , one who is a member of a city characterized by philanthropia, an educated man" (2.5.11). The urbane Dionysophanes and his son Astylus in *Daphnis and Chloe* display much the same combination of urbanity and humanity.

Since something was said earlier about the attitudes that appear in the fifth and fourth centuries B.C., it is perhaps worth making the point here that these feelings turn up again in Greek Romance. Though the noble barbarian does appear, the Greeks for the most part feel that they are superior to the non-Greek foreigner. This attitude springs at least partly from an awareness of urbanity. But it is feelings involving city and country that are most explicitly described. The countryman is not expected to appreciate what is beautiful,[14] and so love which is a special form of such appreciation must remain an urban phenomenon.

Lycaenium in *Daphnis and Chloe* who was originally from the city finds in Daphnis "a rustic simplicity such as she had not expected" (3.18), and her urban awareness eventually overcomes his simple outlook. Viewed from the point of view of an urbanite, this roughness may become an ugliness against which he feels an immediate revulsion. In the *Ephesiaca*, for instance, the worst punishment that Manto can find to inflict upon Anthia is to give her to some boorish goatherd (2.9.2). Again, Clinias in *Clitophon and Leucippe* reacts rather violently to Charicles' betrothal to an ugly woman: "Don't give a beautiful rose to an ugly boor to pick."[15] Perhaps the clearest statement of these feelings is to be found in Dio Chrysostom's *Euboeic Idyll* where the urban sophisticates laugh at the countryman's rough appearance (23) and odd habits (59) and ridicule his simplicity and general boorishness (43).[16]

Before leaving Greek sophistication it must be pointed out that, though Thucydides, Plato, Menander, and the Greek novelists have their own purposes in dealing with Greek urbanity, the phenomenon is essentially the same in each. Pericles and Socrates may be urbane men in ideal situations, and Sostratus may represent urbanity under pressure in a real life context, but as gentlemen they do not differ greatly from one another. At first sight, the urbane man of the romances may appear the exception, but once again any change that is felt comes largely from context and treatment. As literary creations Sostratus and Chaereas may be two completely different phenomena, but in their manners, outlook, and actions they are strikingly similar. To repeat a point made earlier: by the time of the Greek Romance, manners have undergone crystallization and codification, and because the rules are set, the authors have no intention or, for that matter, any need of explicating them. A hero's urbanity is taken for granted and his adventures assume primary importance.

CHAPTER II

EARLY ROMAN
URBANITY

DEVELOPMENTS TO 240 B.C.

Clear traces of any sophistication in Rome before the appearance of Latin literature in 240 B.C. are almost nonexistent, although it is perfectly clear that there must have been a gradual cultural growth in the city almost from the beginning under strong Greek and Etruscan influence. The archaeological evidence leaves the impression that by the time the Republic began Roman, Etruscan, and Greek elements were bound together with the Greco-Etruscan predominating. The balancing of these was to take place in the fifth and fourth centuries B.C. as the Roman element gradually asserted itself.[1]

Though it is impossible to do anything more than guess at details, there are a number of tendencies in this early period which, while they do not prove any high level of refinement, are at least indicative of an emerging cultural sense. The first of these is the exploitation by the Romans of the dramatic forms of people with whom they were coming into contact. Whatever other reasons there may be for their appearance, the adoption of the Fescennine verses from Etruria, the mime from Magna Graecia, and the Atellan farce from Oscan Campania together with the importing of Etruscan actors in 364 B.C. point to an expanding Roman outlook and attempts to satisfy a broader cultural need. But the fact that these were all primitive dramatic amusements with slight literary merit serves as a reminder that the Roman still had quite a way to go in matters of taste.

As they extended their sway over the less-civilized peoples of Italy, the future rulers of the Mediterranean world must have become increasingly conscious that their way of life was culturally superior to that of their neighbors. This second tendency comes partly as a logical assumption, but every now and then there is a hint of such a feeling in the early sections of Livy's *History*. His statement that the earliest Romans looked down upon the Sabines as foreigners (1.17.2)—an attitude which the historian later describes Tarquin (1.35.2-4) and Tanaquil (1.41.3) as opposing— may not be historically reliable, but it represents a logical reconstruction of a situation that probably existed in the early period. The same may be said about the harangue of Canuleius (4.3.10-13) which contains a pointed reference to the foreign origin of Numa, Tarquin, Servius Tullius, and Titus Tatius.

But the account of the speech which Titus Manlius gave in the senate against the Latins in 340 B.C. can be taken a little more seriously.[2] Details must not be pressed, and it is surely to be assumed that the rhetoric is Livy's, but Manlius' objections to the Latins as foreigners who have no rights as far as Roman government and Roman religion are concerned (8.5.8) is probably a true reflection of the fourth century feeling that the Roman was socially superior to his neighbors. Another piece of evidence recorded by the "ancients," as Livy calls them, tends to confirm this. This is the well-known reference to the Gallic opponent of Titus Manlius, who stands stupidly and happily sticking out his tongue (7.10.5). Presumably the contemporary authority found this stupidity and coarseness worth recording because they were characteristics that he as a member of the more civilized Roman society found repulsive.

Another tendency that may be detected in Livy's account of the preliterary period is a gradually increasing rivalry between city and country in which matters of refinement must have played a part. The implication that urban youth and rustic youth are two different groups for purposes of the military draft and the hint that the former are normally called to service before the latter (7.25.8) suggest a gulf that is both political and cultural. On the other hand, because the urban life looked more attractive than a rustic existence, it apparently was tempting the countryman even in this early period to leave his holdings (4.12.7). Livy suggests that matters of refinement are at least part of this difference when in his account of the plague at Rome (3.6.2 f.) he portrays the urbanites as suffering discomfort from the strange and unpleasant odors that result from living at close quarters with the rustics who had flocked to the city.

An episode in the maneuvers near Russellae in 302 B.C. (10.4.7–10) provides what appears to be important evidence for a fairly well-developed Roman urbanity at this time. When the Etruscans masquerade as shepherds in hopes of ambushing the Romans, they are revealed by their accent, bearing, and outward appearance to be city-dwellers rather than true rustics. Evidently the way they talked was the real giveaway, for the Roman general had called forward people "skilled in the language" to pass judgment. While the language was Etruscan and the judges were probably natives of the immediate area, the possibility remains that here in the fourth century B.C. the Romans were sophisticated enough to appreciate the fact that a city-dweller could be recognized from his appearance and his accent. If they were able to do this with Etruscans, there can be no doubt that they were making similar distinctions at Rome.

In addition to the tendencies outlined above, all of which come directly from the history of preliterary times, there is a certain amount of indirect evidence in early Latin literature that must not be overlooked. This is to be found in the vocabulary of sophistication which suggests a continuing Roman refinement that had existed earlier. Words like *facetus* and *scurra* which crop up constantly in connection with urbanity are employed by the early writers with a confidence and a familiarity that hint at a long period of usage. *Facetus* appears in its adverbial form in a fragment of Naevius where it is joined with *defricate*. Though there is no context, the words are probably best translated "cleverly and pungently,"[3] and they take on Roman overtones from the fact of their describing something that was said or done in a satiric manner. This term also appears a number of times in Plautus' plays as adjective and adverb with connotations of politeness and courtesy. *Scurra* turns up first in Plautus, and while his use of the word will be studied in some detail a little later, it is worth noting here that its relatively frequent occurrence—he uses it some seven times—shows that it had been popular for some time.

There can be little doubt, then, that words like *facetus* and *scurra* had had a preliterary history during which they were developing currency in those connotations which Naevius and Plautus adopted. And so they serve as an indication that the Romans were conscious at an early time, probably well before the appearance of literature, of a politeness and perhaps a wittiness (*facetus*), and that they recognized at least one product of such refinement, the *scurra* or man-about-town.[4]

THE EARLY LITERARY PERIOD

The appearance of Latin literature in the middle of the third century before Christ implies the presence of at least some degree of sophistication. To put it another way, the literary mandate given to Livius Andronicus shows "... that the leaders of Roman society ... had come to the conclusion that the usual performances were no longer worthy of the *ludi Romani*, and that something on a higher level should and could be offered to the Roman public: in fact their order was an explicit rejection of any artistic tradition which had existed at Rome till that moment."[5] But it is a mistake to think that the majority of the populace fully understood what an Andronicus, an Accius, a Naevius, or an Ennius was trying to do, for these writers were well ahead of most of their contemporaries in appreciating and interpreting their Greek heritage. Roman culture was just beginning to blossom.

There is no connected account of urbanity in this early period, though Plautus because of the nature and volume of his writing provides much valuable information. The fragments of the works of Naevius, Ennius, Caecilius, and Cato also help. Much of the evidence is scattered and disparate, then, and any account of refinement in the period will necessarily reflect this, but when taken together the topics which follow show clearly that Roman urbanity did exist and that it was exerting an influence on outlook and attitudes.

ROMAN AWARENESS OF GREEK URBANITY

In view of the fact that Greek New Comedy, which had a strong appeal for both playwright and audience at this time, was so liberally spiced with references to and discussion of Greek urbanity, it is more than a little surprising that Plautus' plays only rarely picture such feelings. They are present, however, as a number of examples show. Pardalisca in the *Casina* (649–52), for instance, in a trumped up story of Casina's rage, describes the slave girl's behavior as quite out of keeping with Attic habits (652). Perhaps the maid is implying that Casina as a slave is not entitled to such outbursts, but it is equally possible that she considers them as being inconsistent with the restrained atmosphere that is characteristic of the refined Athenian household.

A similar note of pride marks Saturio's manner in the *Persa* when he exclaims to his daughter that she shall have six hundred jests from his books as a dowry—all of them Attic and not a Sicilian one included (394 f.). These witticisms or *logi,* as Plautus calls them, appear to be the Attic counterpart of the clever, witty, elegantly expressed *urbana dicta* of later times, which are exclusively Roman.[6] The same feeling lies behind Daemones' assertion in the *Rudens* that because he has been born, brought up, and educated in "Attic Athens" he is quite superior to a man from Cyrene.[7]

The attitude expressed here is essentially that which pervades Pericles' funeral oration.

One of the most delightful scenes in the *Miles Gloriosus* (635–68) is that in which Periplectomenus describes himself and his sophistication. As he begins his near-monologue he tells his audience that he is a clever wit (*cavillator facetus*) and an agreeable, tactful guest at table (*conviva commodus*), inasmuch as he always avoids interrupting, never argues with other guests, and knows when to talk and when to keep quiet. Hard upon these lofty pronouncements comes the declaration that he is not a spitter, a noisy throat-clearer, or a snuffler. Rising to a climax, he draws himself up to his full height and states in no uncertain terms that he is a man from Ephesus and no small town Apulian (648). From here he goes on to point out that he is a gracious person who avoids stealing others' girls at the banquet and never monopolizes the meat and drink.

As Periplectomenus rambles on, Plautus' purpose becomes more and more apparent; he is out to satirize the Greek urbanity in the person and words of this character for the enjoyment of his audience. The satire becomes all the more pointed when the eccentric turns to stress his natural versatility. His insistence that he can carry off any part with aplomb—lawyer (severe or mild), dinner guest, parasite, host, or dancer—immediately calls to mind Juvenal's condemnation of the Greeks in Rome for their ability to play any part or do any job, especially the menial.[8]

This passage of the *Miles Gloriosus* shows that Plautus recognized the foreign refinement that was making its way into Rome and that he understood it well enough to present a vivid caricature of one exponent of it. The whole episode has a decidedly Plautine stamp, then; so do the other passages that have been mentioned. As she comments on Attic discipline, Pardalisca raises a chuckle in the Roman audience, since to them Greek life meant excess of one kind or another. Saturio's Attic witticisms and inferior copies from Sicily were also topical for Romans who were not only aware of such sayings, but were fully conscious as well of the differences between the Athenian and the Sicilian Greek cultures.

Further proof that the Romans were coming into contact with the Greek urbanity at this time is furnished by the adjective *barbarus* and its cognates, which Plautus and his contemporaries seem to have adopted with its Greek connotations of foreignness and vulgarity. A fragment of Naevius recalls the division of the world into Hellenes and barbarians,[9] while Caecilius, exploiting the pejorative connotations of the word, associates it with license, ignorance, and stupidity.[10] Perhaps the most familiar instances of this application are to be found in the prologues to the *Asinaria* (11) and the *Trinummus* (19) where the adverb is used to describe Plautus' turning the Greek original "into Latin."[11]

Other evidence for the appearance of Athenian sophistication in Rome at this time is less satisfactory. The discovery of Menander's *Dyscolus* raises interesting speculation about Plautus' play of the same title which has been lost.[12] It is difficult and at the same time dangerous to imagine the Roman piece as being anything like the original, however, since if this were so, it would be quite unlike anything of Plautus which has survived. Among the comedies of Naevius there is one which appears to have been titled *Astiologa*. If this is the correct title, then it provides an indication that the Romans fully appreciated the adjective ἀστεῖος as it related to wit.[13]

Finally, a line and a half of Caecilius' *Titthe* serves not only to confirm the direct transplantation of the feeling from Greece to Rome but also provides a transition to the discussion of city and country. Someone is asking, apparently with sarcasm or incredulity, whether he is to compare his Attic way of life with another's rustic Syrian existence.[14] The point of difference between this man from Athens and the foreigner from across the sea comprises the roughness, the uncouthness, and the rusticity of Syrian life when it is set beside the Athenian refinement.

THE CONTRAST BETWEEN CITY AND COUNTRY

In the discussion between the urban dweller Nicodemus and the old man Dinia at the beginning of Plautus' *Vidularia* (20–55), the differences between an urban and a rustic existence are outlined in broad terms. Life in the country is characterized by difficulty and coarseness, while life in the city is one of sophisticated ease. The city-dweller's pale appearance suggests the indoor life, and hands kept busy with throwing the dice cannot be expected to undertake heavy labor.[15] From this and other contexts it is also clear that the products of these two environments are to keep to themselves. Dinia here cannot believe that Nicodemus wants to be hired as a farm-laborer, while elsewhere Chalinus in the *Casina* (103) mades it amply evident that the countryman Olympio has no reason to be gallivanting about town.

Town and country clash violently at the beginning of the *Mostellaria* (1–83) when Tranio, the urban slave, trades insults with the rustic Grumio. Each to his own way of thinking is perfectly justified in criticizing the other for his manner of living, and as the argument unfolds it becomes clear that there is no common ground between them. Tranio throws boorish habits and home-spun ways in his opponent's face and Grumio quickly retaliates with vitriolic criticism of the man from town. He has no use for the dandy who lives in the city, and he cannot tolerate all the activities that go on there—drinking to excess, wasting money, buying and selling friendly female companions, feeding parasites, giving elaborate banquets, in short, living the dissolute life of the Greeks. Grumio would rather smell like goats and garlic than use imported perfumes and eat exotic foods. Pointed though the rustic's criticism may be, Tranio prevails, for from the moment he catches sight of him, he treats Grumio as a low-life, not only insisting that he get back to the farm, but beating him in the bargain. It is Grumio's task to look after cows. The urban slave complains that his opponent smells of garlic and calls him a piece of filth, a country clod, a goat, a pigsty, and a manure pile. Tranio, of course, is no sophisticated urbanite, but what he says comes from a consciousness of urban standards of refinement.

A delightful bit of banter that passes between Astaphium and Truculentus in the *Truculentus* (257–321) provides further insight into such standards. Plautus has prepared his audience for the irritable rustic with a speech of Astaphium (250–54) in which there is the implication that she as a city-dweller cannot abide such intemperance. During their talk together Truculentus parades his bad temper, and when he resorts to embellishments that involve metaphoric language from the farm, Astaphium shrugs it all off as being straight "barnyardese."[16] The rustic returns the compliment by chiding this young woman of the city for her carefully coifed, perfumed hair and her painted face (286–94). The next time Truculentus appears he seemingly is a changed man (673–98), for he claims to have become a wit and a connoisseur of fine repartee. What he says here is worth noticing not only because it relates refined humor or wit to urban life, but also because it leaves the strong implication that a period of living in town can be expected to remove rusticity.

The question of whether in these Plautine contexts this contrast between city and country and the attitudes arising from it are Greek or Roman is a difficult one to answer. Mention of the Panathenaic festival and Athena's peplos leaves no doubt about the atmosphere at the beginning of the *Mercator*. In other places, however, where the scene is not specified, even though the episode may be Greek-inspired, it would be perfectly natural for the Roman audience in their minds to shift action and attitudes to a Roman and Italian setting. Strabax' triumphal march into the city to do battle with the city dandies in the *Truculentus* (645–63), for example, could easily be taken as Roman, especially since mention of Tarentum and Mars gives the whole scene an Italian flavor. The environment in which the *Mostellaria* begins is assumed to be Greek, but two instances of the verb *pergraecari* (22, 64) inject a Roman orientation. The atmosphere never becomes completely Roman, however, for Plautus boldly complicates the issue by mentioning Attica (30) and the Piraeus (66) as places figuring in the action.[17]

The situation in the two passages of the *Truculentus* is much clearer. When Astaphium meets the irritable rustic for the first time, the audience is startled by a Latin pun. The young lady's broad pronunciation of *iram* as *eiram* has caused Truculentus to hear *eam*. Moreover, during their second encounter the two begin quibbling about the Latin language in a discussion which contains ridicule of the Praenestines who were a favorite object of Roman satire at this time. When these Roman overtones are noticed, the word *urbs* as it it used here (682) raises interesting possibilities. The question of whether this connotes Rome or Athens cannot be answered with any certainty, but it is possible that the process by which the term was becoming equated with Rome is reflected here.[18]

A consideration of the vocabulary that is used by Plautus to designate what belongs to city and country is also instructive. The abstracts *urbanitas* and *rusticitas* have not yet made their appearance, but the adjectives *urbanus*, *rusticus*, and *agrestis* occur often enough to show that Roman refinement is growing. While Plautus may employ *agrestis* in a relatively straightforward manner to describe an aspect of the rustic scene, he also uses it to underline the dullness, roughness, and irritability of an ignorant countryman like Truculentus (253).[19]

Rusticus occurs with similarly pejorative connotations, at times in contexts of opposition between city and country. Tranio throws it out in the *Mostellaria* (40), for instance, to conjure up the rudeness, filth, and barnyard smells of the boorish life of a Grumio. Again, Sophoclidisca uses it in a similarly depreciatory way in the *Persa* (169) where it is related to ignorance, thoughtlessness, and fatuity, so that it has almost become a synonym of *bardus* with its overtones of dullness and stupidity. It is important to notice that the extension in the meaning of these adjectives has taken place from the point of view of the city-dweller who considers his life and its trappings to be infinitely more refined than what he sees in the country.

A more positive statement of this feeling occurs in a scene from the *Mercator* (712–19) where urbanite and rustic are contrasted once again. When Dorippa, who is angry and out of sorts, fails to return Lysimachus' greeting, he muses to himself, "Well now, are city people turning into rustics?" From what he says here it is clear that the urban dweller is expected to show good manners at all times and that part of these is a characteristic courtesy that is lacking in a man from the country. It is impossible to say whether the standards of urbanity that are implied here are essentially Greek or Roman, but it does not really matter, for the fact of the appearance of a discussion involving politeness and courtesy in which the thoroughly Roman terms *urbanus* and *rusticus* are used shows that the Romans must have been aware of such matters.

In view of the nuances of rudeness, roughness, and boorishness that seem to be clustering about *agrestis* and *rusticus* at this time, it is perhaps worth asking as a final footnote whether *urbanus* had taken on the contrasting connotations of culture and urbanity. The answer seems to be that the term does not yet have the meanings "urbane," "refined," and "citified" that are current in later writers, though it is apparently moving in that direction. Its alliance with words of elegance and love in the *Truculentus* (658) and its association with *scurra* in the *Mostellaria* (15) and the *Trinummus* (202) bring the adjective into line with the smartness, cleverness, and refinement of the city.[20]

THE *Scurra*

Through most of Latin literature the *scurra* is an extreme and not very admirable product of the refinement that characterizes urban life, and his appearance in Plautus' plays is no exception. When Grumio uses the word in the *Mostellaria* (15) to reproach

Tranio for twisting one of his remarks, it is clear that he means to equate him with a clever, popular, always suspect man-about-town. In the *Trinummus* (202) Megaronides speaks of "ever-present urban citizens whom they call *scurrae*." These characters seem to be gossips who profess to know everything, even the innermost thoughts of men, though they actually know nothing. They have all the brass and lack of respect for the truth that typifies such individuals and couple this with a complete disregard for the person or thing they are praising or blaming. A large part of this characterization seems to be Plautus' own, since purely Roman elements have been discovered in it.[21]

When this description is compared with a digression in the *Curculio* (462–84), the *scurra* takes on new dimensions. Here the *choragus* is describing various types that are to be found in the city, and as he does so, he mentions a group that haunts the area about the *Lacus Curtius*. They are brash, bold characters who are always chattering and hurling their vicious insults at others without cause or reason, though they themselves are the ones that deserve criticism (477ff.). While the speaker does not name this crowd, they seem to have much in common with Megaronides' *scurrae*.[22]

The occurrence of *urbanus* qualifying *scurra* in the lines from the *Mostellaria* and *Trinummus* is quite surprising, since the noun is itself a city word and normally needs no such explication. Perhaps there is simply a colloquial redundancy here, but it seems more likely that the *scurra* needs such qualification because he is a character that is making his influence felt in the city for the first time.[23] Indeed, there may be some attempt to isolate and define the type in what Megaronides says. However this may be, the appearance of the *scurra* in Plautus' plays not only argues for the presence of a Roman urbanity with recognizable standards, but suggests as well that urban life is now producing people who have carried such feelings to extremes.

ROMAN ATTITUDES

The attitude of the more refined urbanite towards the boorish-ness of the rustic has already been mentioned. There are two other groups of people about whom the Romans had similar feelings at this time—the Greeks, who were making their influence felt in the city more strongly than ever before, and the inhabitants of the towns and countryside of Italy, many of whom had been subjects of Rome for some time. Cato's opposition to the Greeks is well known, and much of it must have stemmed from a conviction that Rome had an identity of her own and that part of this identity was a refinement worth fostering. This is no doubt one of the reasons that he objected so strenuously to the Greeks' calling the Romans barbarous.[24] Plautus also felt this way, for Periplectomenus' mono-logue in the *Miles Gloriosus* (635–68) which was discussed earlier represents a criticism of Greek standards of refinement by a Roman who felt his were superior. In other Plautine contexts this feeling appears in words like *congraeco* and *pergraecor*, perhaps coined for the occasion to emphasize aspects of Greek sophistication that the Roman could not abide.[25]

There is more specific comment on the people living in Italy, partly because by this time Rome had had much intercourse with them and partly because, as Cato's *Origines* shows, the Romans had developed a genuine interest in their fellow Italians. The reali-zation that differences existed came as early as Naevius who in his *Apella* apparently lashed out at the boorish Apulians.[26] This in turn immediately calls to mind Plautus' snap at these people, par-ticularly those of Animula.[27] But the Roman was most outspoken about people and places much closer to home. In an amusing bit of dialogue in the *Captivi* (880–85), Cora, Praeneste, Signia, Frusino, and Alatrium are called barbarian cities by Hegio, while Ergasilus describes them as rough and wild like Hegio's meals. The passage is Plautus' own and shows that he felt the refined urban life to be superior to the rough and ready rustic life of towns not very far away.

The Praenestines were a favorite subject for criticism by the Romans in this early period. In a fragment of Naevius' *Ariolus*, a speaker who is perhaps from the city insists that good urban cooking should not be wasted on people from Praeneste and Lanuvium, since they are accustomed to rather simple, uncouth, rustic fare like sow's belly and nuts.[28] Elsewhere the censure of the Praenestines for their boasting brings with it the implication that the Roman was refined enough to recognize and avoid such excesses.[29]

But it was the Praenestine speech that seems to have bothered Romans like Plautus the most, as two pointed references to the Latin spoken by these people show. When Callicles asks Stasimus in the *Trinummus* when a certain betrothal took place, the slave answers: "Right here in front of the house, *tammodo* as the man from Praeneste puts it" (608f.). If Stasimus' remark is put together with the observation of Festus the grammarian that *tammodo* was an archaic form for *modo*,[30] then it seems clear that the Praenestines are being criticized for using outdated Latin. This may, of course, be another reflection of their rusticity.

In an episode from the *Truculentus* Astaphium pounces upon Truculentus for using the form *rabo* rather than the more normal *arrabo*. The rustic takes the opportunity to display his new urbane wit as he informs her that the *a* is superfluous, and if the Praenestines can say *conia* rather than *ciconia*, then he can use *rabo* (687–91). It has been suggested that the Praenestines were prone to leave out vowels so that they originally pronounced this word *c'conia* which soon became *conia* because it was virtually impossible to hear the double consonant.[31] However this may be, it is clear that Plautus is using the rustic Truculentus to poke fun at the way the Praenestines pronounced certain Latin words. Just as the informed Roman took exception to the boorish habits and tastes of the Italians with whom he came into contact, so he could not abide Latin that was not up-to-date and not pronounced correctly.

ENNIUS' PORTRAIT OF AN URBANE ROMAN

From what has already been said it is perfectly obvious that the Roman of the third and second centuries before Christ not only was aware of his urbanity but was making judgments from it. An attempt to find this urbane man in the literature of the period leads directly to the lengthy fragment of Ennius' *Annales* in which the poet is describing the habits and personality of the Roman whom Servilius Geminus is about to consult.[32] While there is no discussion of urbanity as such, the emphasis on learning, restraint, and propriety shows that it is very much part of Ennius' thinking. The man is an attractive person (*suavis homo*), and is contented, happy, and wise (*scitus*). At the head of his good qualities is a certain culture (*doctus*) which along with his learning and his finesse displays itself in what he says and how he says it. He is a man of few words who not only says the right thing at the right time, but also knows when to speak up and when to keep silent. The emphasis on sophisticated conversation marked by a variety of topics and a proper wit is a clear anticipation of Cicero's observations on the way a sophisticated Roman of his time is expected to express himself. While Ennius includes much more in his discussion of this anonymous Roman, it is impossible to miss the urbanity that pervades the man's character and governs his actions and outlook.

CHAPTER III

THE SCIPIONIC PERIOD

The intensification of Roman interest in Greek cultural values that marked the second century B.C. resulted in an even greater awareness of Greek urbanity than before. There are abundant examples of the process at work. According to Horace,[1] Lucilius was dependent, at least to some extent, on Greek Old Comedy, and it is a well-known fact that Terence found inspiration in the writers of New Comedy, especially Menander. Again, not only was Scipio so drawn to Xenophon's *Cyropedia* that he apparently never let it out of his hands,[2] but Plato's Socrates also had a strong appeal for this sophisticate and his contemporaries.[3] It has already been noticed that each of these models—Old Comedy, New Comedy, Xenophon, and Socrates—in one way or another reflects the classical Greek refinement.

Among the more important contemporary Greek influences affecting Roman urbanity were the writings of the Stoic philosopher Panaetius, who was an intimate of Scipio and the other learned men of the period. "It is difficult to exaggerate the influence of Panaetius, not merely on Roman Stoicism, of which he is the real founder, but also on Roman law, social and political theory, and through his grammatical and rhetorical interests upon the Roman literary theory and composition."[4] His importance as far as Roman refinement is concerned may be seen from the first book of Cicero's *De Officiis* where a large part of the discussion is devoted to decorum and propriety.[5] In what appears to be Panaetius' definition (96),[6] this propriety is described as involving a harmony with nature out of which come restraint and self-control accompanied by a certain gentlemanly attitude and appearance (*cum specie quadam liberali*). There is, of course, much more under discussion here than urbanity, but the adjective *liberalis* shows that this is included in the philosopher's thinking.

A little later Panaetius returns to this aspect of decorum when he insists that all of a person's habits—walking, sitting, reclining, facial expression, movement of the hands—must be in conformity with nature. A man must avoid overreacting to the point of effeminacy, but he must not be so disinterested and neglectful as to leave an impression of roughness and boorishness (128f.). Although the *urbanus homo* is not mentioned specifically, his counterparts, the hyperurbane man and the rustic, lurk behind the scenes.

It was noticed earlier that a man's urbanity is best revealed by the way in which he expresses himself, and if the first book of Cicero's *De Officiis* is a faithful reflection of Panaetius' original, then it is clear that the philosopher spent some time describing proper conversation. Not every detail of the discussion of wit (103f.) can be attributed to him, as the evidence of Ciceronian adaptation shows, but from the context it is apparent that Panaetius warned against jesting that ran to excess and could not abide the man who exhibited a coarse, ungentlemanly sense of humor.

What the philosopher says here anticipates the more detailed discussion of the constituents of proper conversation[7] which appears a little later (1.133–37). Detailed analysis of this section will be put off to the next chapter, since many of the ideas are important to Cicero's concept of an *urbanus homo*, but Panaetius' emphasis on propriety of wit, subject matter, and length of conversation must be mentioned here. Moreover, the fact that the philosopher chose the "Socratics" as the best examples of proper discourse is extremely important, for with this observation he relates his ideas on correct conversation to the Greek urbanity as it was displayed by Plato's Socrates. This does not mean, however, that the urbanity of the

36

De Officiis is to be taken as a faithful reflection of sophistication, for Panaetius is presenting a philosophical or universal refinement which stems from a proper, ethical, Stoic view of life.

Because these tenets were philosophically based, sophisticates like Scipio and Laelius could accept them without worrying that the Greek urbanity would overwhelm the Roman. For this reason too Cicero was able to use Panaetius' remarks to elaborate his views on Roman urbanity. It may be going too far to insist that Livy's description of Scipio in his *History* (28.18.6) shows the influence that Panaetius exerted in matters of refinement, but it does at least suggest what the practical connection might have been between his thinking and the Roman urbanity as it was displayed by a man like Scipio. The gentleman as he appears here is quite charming and affable and has a quick and ready genius. This pleasant personality combines with the eloquence that the situation demands to enable the Roman to win over even the most hostile barbarian with no trouble at all.

But this strong interest in the influence from the Greek is only one tendency of the times. There is no missing the accompanying antithetical feeling that the native Roman culture should be preserved, fostered, and protected. One of the problems that had to be faced, then, was that of combining the adopted and adapted Greek with Roman ideas and feelings to produce a culture and a refinement which was peculiarly Roman. This bipartition in Roman thinking is represented in literature by Terence and Lucilius, for the playwright shows an absorption with humanizing and refining influences from Greece, while Lucilius balances him precisely with frequent confident expression of Roman values. In Terence's plays Greek moods, Greek thoughts, Greek ideas have been carefully prepared for Roman consumption via the *sermo purus* so that the urbanity of his subject matter is Greek, while the urbanity of his language is Roman. In Lucilius' *Satires,* though the poet is fully aware of his Greek heritage, the Roman moods, Roman thoughts, and Roman and Italian ideas make his urbanity, whether it be in

37

form or content, strictly Roman. For these reasons both writers deserve careful consideration.

If present scholarly judgment is correct, then Terence was apparently writing for a sophisticated minority.[8] For this and other reasons as well, he made a conscious effort to retain the spirit of the originals by putting his characters in a Greek metropolis and keeping them there without softening the foreign atmosphere and coloring at all.[9] In spite of the fact that it is generally agreed that Terence is in this way faithful to his models, the precise relationship between the Roman and Greek plays is yet to be determined. This problem of originality has an important bearing on a search for urbanity in the plays, but there is no point in reopening the question here. It is simpler to begin from the generally accepted premise that Terence's plays are relatively accurate reflections of Greek New Comedy and search in each instance for criteria that will indicate whether the particular allusion is purely Greek or whether it is colored by a Roman outlook.

At a number of points in the plays Terence presents an urban-rustic contrast. In the *Eunuchus* Laches observes that by having his country place near town he never becomes bored with either city or countryside (971 ff.), since whenever he tires of the one he can easily move to the other. This character is a sophisticated Athenian gentleman who, because he is quite aware of the difference between the urban and rustic environments, is fully determined to enjoy the best of each. There is nothing in these lines to suggest anything but a straight transfer of thought from the original. The same may be said of a scene in the *Hecyra* between Sostrata and Pamphilus. The son's reaction to his mother's desire to retreat to the country is one of disbelief accompanied by the implication that moving to the rustic atmosphere is a kind of exile for the city-dweller.[10]

A search for the gentleman in Terence's plays leads directly to a scene in the *Andria* (55–60) where Simo gives an idea of what is expected of an urbane man. Though most of this breed devote themselves wholeheartedly either to horses, hounds, and hunting or to attending the lectures of the philosophers, the young Pamphilus has gone to neither of these extremes but has indulged in both with admirable restraint. The situation here immediately calls to mind the scenes in Aristophanes' *Clouds* in which the young Pheidippides is portrayed as giving himself up completely, first to the ephemeral attractions of a life of luxury in Athens and then to the reactionary teachings of Socrates. There seems to be little difference between the standards of conduct implicitly recommended by Aristophanes and those praised by Terence.

To this point the evidence offered by Terence could hardly be called remarkable. But even a quick glance at the *Adelphoe* raises more hopeful prospects, for here the action revolves around the contrasting habits and outlook of city-dweller and rustic. The antithesis between Micio, the smooth, sophisticated, generous urbanite and Demea, the harsh, thrifty, irritable countryman, is carefully drawn from the opening soliloquy in which Micio outlines the differences between his peaceful, easygoing urban existence and Demea's frugal, almost niggardly life of trial and tribulation.[11]

Many of the same sentiments come from Demea himself later when he pits the affability and ease of life in the city where leisure and banqueting fill the day against the rough, rustic life which tends to produce only unwholesome characteristics in countrymen like himself (860–67). Terence never lets his audience forget this contrast; he cannot afford to, since it motivates most of the action of the play. In the latter passage Demea offers a concise but complete self-analysis (866): *ego ille agrestis, saevos, tristis, parcus, truculentus, tenax.* He is a man of the earth, then, and he is rough around the edges, possessing a gloomy, frugal view of life that makes him not only stingy, but also hard to get along with. Demea's idealizing of the rustic frugality and sobriety is rather grotesque and recalls Cnemon's similarly strange sense of values as it unfolds in the *Dyscolus.* It is no wonder that with this kind of background and outlook Terence's rustic becomes a completely objectionable character in the eyes of those with whom he comes into contact.

Most of the traits that Demea attributes to himself in his one line characterization make their appearance or exert their influence at some point in the play. His pessimistic outlook precedes him onto the stage: "Why so gloomy?" Micio says to him, even before he has opened his mouth (82). This attitude is also exhibited by Ctesipho, the country-reared son (267). Micio describes Demea as harsh beyond what is just and fair (64) and paints his sphere of influence as an *imperium* (66) which he governs through fear (75 ff.). Micio also implies that he is an irritable old man (60–63), and Demea confirms this impression at his first appearance with his ungracious and perfunctory greeting. Whether he has suddenly become aware of the fact that Ctesipho may not be all innocence (355–60), whether he is confused by what is going on at a particular time (544–47), whether he is telling what will happen to Ctesipho's girl when he gets her on the farm (845–49), or whether he is getting his own back at the end of the play, he is consistent in his irritability. In fact, at times this bad temper drives him to the brink of madness (111). There is also a rustic simplicity about Demea which manifests itself most obviously in the gulling he undergoes at the hands of Syrus, and it is this characteristic that makes him a delightfully comic character.

Out of this combination of sternness, irritability, and simplicity comes a final rustic trait—a thoroughly unreasoned, boorish obstinacy. This asserts itself frequently in the play, but nowhere as clearly as when Demea appears before Micio's house after tramping all over Rome trying to follow Syrus' directions. Though he is reeling from exhaustion, he damns Syrus and informs the audience that he is going to besiege the house until Micio returns (713–18). It is no wonder, then, that Demea appears out of place in the city and falls so far short of being able to understand the point of view of his urban counterpart. Ctesipho has found the townsman Aeschinus to lead him through the labyrinth of city ways, but Demea has no one. He is always questioning what Micio does (60–63), and he cannot see why the urbanite is so philosophic about what is happening around him (758–62). As a matter of fact, he is ashamed of his brother (391 f.). It is only when he decides to adopt Micio's outlook and methods that he begins to assume the upper hand.

Micio is just the opposite of Demea in most respects. Because of his soft, leisure-filled life in town, he is easygoing and completely at peace with the world. Not only does he carefully avoid giving offense, but he usually has a smile for everyone he meets (863f.). Although Micio is nowhere described in so many words as a gentleman, he comes close to depicting himself as such in his opening soliloquy where he mentions that his sense of parental discipline involves a moderate, kindly, and gentlemanly approach to life (*pudore et liberalitate*). This he contrasts with Demea's rustic philosophy of training and teaching through fear (57f.), so that while the rustic's byword is *metus*, Micio applies friendship (67) and generosity (72). Indeed, the fact that this gentleman is generous even to an extreme is one of the most important complicating factors in the play. The climax of his indulgence comes when he gives in to the idea of taking a wife (944f.) after only slight protest. Throughout this scene his behavior is remarkably like that of Callippides in the *Dyscolus* who agrees to a similar demand with a minimum of argument.

Micio reveals his urbanity at almost every turn in the *Adelphoe*. His first encounter with Demea rather strikingly parallels the initial meeting between Sostratus and Gorgias in the *Dyscolus*. When the rustic comes storming on and plunges ungraciously *in medias res*, Micio's first reaction is to greet him discreetly and urbanely: *salvom te advenire, Demea,/gaudemus* (8of.). While Demea goes on to rave about Aeschinus and his adventures, his urbane opponent offers rebuttal, but never loses his composure for a moment. After Demea's departure, however, Micio lets down his guard and reveals that he is really quite worried by what he has heard (141–54). In the whole play there is actually only one place where he loses control of his emotions, but even here his irritation at Demea for insisting that he take a wife (934–45) loses some of its force, since it comes in the wake of the rustic's more violent pronouncements.

Not only is Micio the gentleman restrained and reserved, but he is also marked by a natural cleverness which is in direct contrast to Demea's rustic simplicity. This is perhaps best exemplified by the subtle, witty joke that he plays on Aeschinus (635–83). Micio may be out to teach the young man a lesson and it is possible that Aeschinus learns something from the ruse, but, no matter what purposes and results are involved, the story Micio contrives and the reasoning he employs stem from his refinement. Not only is it the whim of a man from town to fabricate a tale like this, but there is no mean intent in Micio's treatment of Aeschinus. His motives are to be contrasted with those of the slave Syrus as he sends Demea scurrying about town.

In the *Adelphoe*, then, Terence presents a fairly complete picture of the rustic and his boorishness and of the townsman and his refinement. But, as so often with Roman New Comedy, the question of originality remains. It has already been indicated that a complete solution to this problem is all but impossible, since much more work needs to be done on the relationship between Terence and his models. But a comparison with the fragments of Menander's *Adelphoe* and with his *Dyscolus* provides some basis for deciding whether these portraits are Terence's or whether they are essentially what he found in Greek New Comedy. There are not many external indications of similarities or differences between the *Adelphoe* of Terence and the Menandrian original. Donatus records one difference in characterization when he hints that Demea at his first appearance in the Roman play (81) is more irascible than Menander's character had been,[12] though it is almost impossible to say whether Terence made his character consistently more irritable throughout the play.

A comparison between the rustic's estimate of himself (866) and the Greek line from which this comes reveals that in both cases Demea is a product of the country (*agrestis, ἄγροικος*), hard to get along with (*truculentus*, πικρός), and niggardly (*tenax*, φειδωλός). For the hard work (ἐργάτης) of the original, Terence seems to have substituted frugality (*parcus*), while the sullen irritability of Menander's Demea (σκυθρός) has become a fierceness (*saevos*) and a gloominess (*tristis*).[13] A glance at individual words, then, may suggest that the Latin rustic is a less restrained character than the Greek, but a comparison of the two lines as a whole which takes into account the different meters and the fact that Terence is striving for a parallelism that is not present in the Greek fragment tends to make the difference less significant.[14]

With the one qualification mentioned by Donatus, Rieth in his penetrating study of the *Adelphoe* seems to take Demea in the play as being essentially what he was in the Greek original. He feels that even the dramatic action of the third act is basically Menander's, though in the middle of it Demea utters a typically Roman complaint about the degeneration of the good, old time-honored mores.[15] Some may also agree with Rieth that there is a typically Roman pride in Demea's final speech,[16] but such a point of view necessitates accepting this speech and so the ending of the play as Terentian, and this it is impossible to do. For the German scholar, then, Terence's countryman may be a little more irritable than Menander's and he may have the odd "Romanism" put into his mouth, but, in spite of these differences, Demea is essentially what he was in the Greek play.

Rieth feels that Micio too is a faithful transferral from the Greek and that his thoughts belong to Menander's time. Because he is not to be paralleled in Plautus, he is something new to Rome and represents a new epoch in Latin literature.[17] Plautus had put the urbane Greek forward for purposes of ridicule, while Terence seems to have brought Micio into Roman literature because he represented thoughts and actions that were worthy of study by Romans interested in matters of refinement.

A comparison between the *Adelphoe* and the *Dyscolus* tends to confirm Rieth's feelings regarding these two characters. The plays are quite different in a number of important respects, since the *Dyscolus* is a relatively candid examination of the problems of city and country in fourth century Athens, while the *Adelphoe* is a study of two diametrically opposed theories of parental discipline which the playwright cleverly hangs on two characters that are easily contrasted in background and outlook. Moreover, although the themes of both plays move on the level of the universal, the action of the *Dyscolus* is closely tied to Athens, while that of the *Adelphoe* could relate to pretty well any urban center. Another obvious, though important, difference between the two comedies is to be noticed in the fact that, while Sostratus and his fellow urbanites have moved to the country, Demea and Micio are active in the city.

But no matter what general differences may be found, they are all overshadowed by the striking parallels that exist between the characters of the two plays. The fathers Micio and Callippides are both marked by an indulgence which springs from their extreme refinement. When Micio is being pressed to take a wife (*Ad.* 929–45) and Callippides is being asked to give his approval to the marriages (*Dysc.* 783–820), each father, after what seems to be too brief and not too strenuous an expression of unwillingness, becomes completely agreeable to an idea that would normally require lengthy thought and consideration. Demea, of course, finds a parallel in Cnemon, for they have irritability, niggardliness, stubbornness, and a general lack of any comprehension of city ways in common. Moreover, as rustics they are both foils for the urbane characters that appear in the plays. But there is an obvious difference between them, since Cnemon is a full-fledged misanthrope, while Demea simply has misanthropic tendencies. Terence's rustic cannot be an out-and-out cynic or there would be no dialogue between him and Micio and so no possibility of compromise at the end of the *Adelphoe.*[18]

It should be noted in passing that Aeschinus finds a counterpart in Sostratus and Ctesipho in Gorgias. Just as Sostratus is impotent in the country and needs the help of Gorgias to attain his purposes, so Ctesipho is similarly out of place in town and has to rely on Aeschinus for aid. It would be dangerous to press these parallels any further, but the conclusion to be drawn from the comparison is obvious. No matter how they are viewed, the actions and characters of the *Adelphoe* are essentially those of the Greek New Comedy.

The difference in outlook between Terence and Lucilius has already been mentioned. While the playwright chose a Greek form, Lucilius was at work developing an original genre in which the point of view was strictly Roman and the subject matter was drawn from Rome and Italy. The satirist fully understood the Greek culture, but his appreciation of it was more akin to that exhibited by Plautus than by Terence, for while he allowed himself to be influenced by the foreign material, he felt that re-evaluation, criticism, and improvement of what was Roman were just as important. In Terence's comedies interest in raising the level of Roman culture is implicit, but in Lucilius' *Satires* there is full and clear expression of this concern.

The satirist's well-known comment on Titus Albucius suggests the limits that the author and, presumably, many of his contemporaries would put on the civilizing influence from across the Adriatic.[19] Throughout this fragment, Lucilius maintains a contrast between Albucius with his Hellenomania on the one hand and people and institutions that are thoroughly Italian on the other, whether it be a Roman or Sabine townsman, centurion, standard-bearer, praetor, lictor, or a troop of men (*turma*). What he cannot abide is the fact that this creature has turned his back on the good old rustic virtues that have made Rome and Romans what they are.

Two other fragments that are usually associated with this one (84–86M) show that matters of urbanity may be part of Lucilius' thinking as he moves to the attack. In the one the writer sarcastically describes Albucius' rhetorical use of Greek as charmingly arranged words (*lexis*) placed like tiny tesserae in a mosaic to form a precious and intricate pattern, while in the second fragment he draws a contrast between the thoroughly Roman Crassus and Albucius whom he calls "too full of [Greek] rhetoric" (*rhetoricoterus*). Lucilius has no use for Albucius' Grecizing simply because one of the main purposes of the cultured Roman of these times was to keep his speech and writing as pure as possible by protecting it from excessive outside influence,[20] a process which had gained considerably greater momentum by Ciceronian times.

Lucilius' criticism of Albucius calls to mind a fragment from a speech of Scipio preserved by Macrobius[21] where the speaker is deploring the fact that children from a tender age are taught habits that were avoided by their forebears. Singing and dancing with less than reputable companions come in for special criticism, and mention of the sambuca, psalterium, and crotalum which accompany these musical activities points to Greek inspiration. The old Roman mores are under siege and Scipio, perhaps the leading Hellenophile of his time, is quick to defend them against a Greek influence that he considers excessive.

There are indications in the *Satires* of an opposition to potentially undermining influences from other directions as well. Lucilius' criticism of the Lydians for the way they dress (12M), whether it be his own comment or quotation of another's view,[22] contains clear contempt for one non-Roman group and its habits. He strikes much the same note in his censure of the interest-pinching Syrophoenician.[23] It should be noticed in passing that the source of such feelings was only partly a sense of urbanity, for it was also a strong patriotism and a desire to protect the moral fibre of the Romans that produced this contempt.

In other contexts it is possible to hear Lucilius the urbane man of Rome speaking. He is thoroughly aware, for instance, of the urban-rustic contrast and seems to have paid considerable attention to it in his poetry. In some instances, like Aristophanes, he uses the country as a positive example in criticizing undesirable urban habits.[24] But Lucilius' view of the rustic is by no means always positive or even neutral. In the Satire on Troginus' dinner party, for example, a good old dull rustic appears babbling away with the others,[25] at least part of whom have the smell of the barnyard about them.[26] Just as he laughs at this "banquet" with its rustic overtones, so in another satire Lucilius evidently made fun of rustic fare. The only indication that such a poem existed is to be found in Charisius' comment that Lucilius, in his Book Five, derides a rustic meal.[27] Although this statement has been questioned by some who seem to feel that Lucilius would not have ridiculed the rustic,[28] there is no good reason for not taking it at face value. After all, the poet was an outspoken *urbanus homo*, and the rustics were always at the mercy of the sophisticated critic. What is more, this kind of satire focusing on rustic fare is in a direct line from Naevius' treatment of the boorish eating habits of the Praenestines and Lanuvians. The tradition, then, was well established.

Mention of the Praenestines serves as a reminder that Lucilius criticized them in much the same way as his predecessors had. According to Quintilian (1.5.56), the satirist attacked a certain Vettius for using Etruscan, Sabine, and Praenestine words. Perhaps dialectal variants in Vettius' speech are under criticism here,[29] but the censure in all probability includes more than mere words. The parallel that Quintilian draws between the satirist's comments and those of Asinius Pollio on Livy's *Patavinitas* suggests that the whole flavor of Vettius' speech, including not only vocabulary but also pronunciation and tone of voice, is under discussion.[30] It is more than simple coincidence that this passage from the *Satires* has been connected with Cicero's mention of the accent of Quintus Valerius in the *De Oratore* (3.43) where the discussion centers around a proper pronunciation and tone of voice, a combination which, as will be shown in the next chapter, produced an *urbanitas* of speech.[31] If Cichorius is correct in making this association, then it is not preposterous to suggest that Lucilius is using *urbanitas* as a basis for his criticism of Vettius.

The fragment in which the satirist mocks the speech of a certain Caecilius points in the same direction.[32] Even a quick reading of these words leaves the clear impression that the man is being criticized for exhibiting at least one rustic characteristic—the pronunciation of the diphthong *ae* as a long, flat *e.* The implication in *rusticus* is that Caecilius is a boor, and another fragment that is generally taken as referring to this magistrate hints that this boorishness went beyond his speech.[33] If the person under discussion is Gaius Caecilius Metellus Caprarius, who was *consul designatus* for the year 117/16 B.C., as many people think, then it is also possible that Lucilius somewhere in this satire capitalized on the man's name to make a special point of his rusticity. It is important to notice that, since the Caecilii were linked with Praeneste by at least one tradition, what the satirist says is probably a reflection of the Roman attitude expressed earlier by Naevius and Plautus. In each case the disapproval stems from an awareness of what constitutes Roman urbanity.[34] Two further conclusions may be drawn from this line. In the first place, there must have been fairly clear recognition at this time of an *urbanus sermo* which included not only a correct vocabulary and proper use of it, but a careful, urban and urbane pronunciation. Because he does not have it, Caecilius deserves to be laughed at.

In another fragment, Lucilius may be providing a glimpse of how the *urbani* of his time were attempting to refine this pronunciation when he smiles at Scipio for using *pertisum* instead of *pertaesum*[35] in order to appear more refined and clever (*facetior*). The poet cannot accept this, and his reason for disapproving seems to be that Scipio's pronunciation of the word is exaggerated as far in the direction of hyperurbanity as Caecilius' long *e* was in the direction of rusticity.

The use of *rusticus* in combination with *pretor* in this line leads to a second conclusion. There can be no doubt that Lucilius is using the word quite unexpectedly for *urbanus,* and since it here has the double connotation of a neutral "rustic" and a negative "countryfied" or "boorish," then *urbanus* which would be the proper and official designation should logically connote both "urban" and "urbane." It is entirely possible, then, that this adjective has developed such an extension in meaning by this time, but since it does not yet appear with such overtones clearly implied, it is safer not to press the point. It is fair to conclude, however, that Lucilius' use of *rusticus* shows that *urbanus* is at least undergoing an extension in meaning.[36]

This is the evidence, then, fragmentary and tantalizing though it may be, that Lucilius has to offer for urbanity.[37] There remains the task of appraising his testimony and that of Terence to try to determine the true state of refinement in this period. If a half century or so earlier Plautus and other sophisticated Romans were conscious of an *urbanitas*, it would be natural to expect an even greater awareness in Scipionic times. In Terence there is direct transfer from the Greek with some, though apparently minimal, Romanization. But Terence was not simply copying, for the vehicle he used to bring his material before his audience was the *sermo purus* of Rome and the language of his plays is a reflection of the *urbanus sermo* that marked the gentleman and his urbanity.[38] Terence's comedies reflect a Greek urbanity in subject matter and a Roman urbanity of language which have not yet undergone the assimilation that marks the Ciceronian and Horatian *urbanitas*. It is entirely possible that this layering of Greek and Roman refinement was among the characteristics that made Terence's plays less popular than those of Plautus.

But it is dangerous to put too much emphasis on the apparent lack of assimilation, for modern experiments on the stage have shown that a complete unity is not necessary for a successful production. Moreover, even though he adapted the subject matter very little, Terence made it easier for his audience to reconcile it, at least in part, with their own experience, by choosing his models very carefully. In the *Adelphoe*, the scene, characters, and situation may all be Greek, but the question of harshness and laxity in child-rearing was something that the Romans could appreciate, especially the sophisticated minority to whom the play was addressed.

49

Micio would catch the interest of a thoughtful spectator as a type that had not yet been fully and sympathetically dealt with on the Roman stage, while Demea would strike home at once as being a rustic type familiar to the playgoers because of their association with Italian and Roman rustics. The rivalry between city and country would also be topical, for the gulf between the two was now felt to be greater than ever before. Demea probably served as a catalyst which made it easier for the Roman audience to accept the matter of the play.

Lucilius was not so much interested in searching for new ideas of urbanity as he was determined to explicate what had already been established as Roman. In trying to protect and improve what he considered to be the true *urbanitas* by working from within, he was in the tradition of Plautus. It is impossible to know with any certainty whether *urbanitas* as Lucilius conceived of it was a more fully developed phenomenon than it was in Plautus' time, but the fact that the vocabulary of refinement had evolved semantically suggests some change in that direction.

Mention has already been made of the extension in meaning of the word *urbanus,* which is implied in Lucilius' gibe at Caecilius. His use of *barbarus* to designate non-Romans such as a Lusitanian Viriathus and a Carthaginian Hannibal[39] points to the fact that in matters of sophistication the Roman was setting himself off from others whom he felt to be inferior in much the same way as the Greeks had dissociated themselves from foreign and barbarian elements. Perhaps this usage reflects a Greek influence, but it is equally possible that the Romans' sense of refinement and sophistication had reached the point where *barbarus* could be naturally applied in this way without any impetus from outside. This word is actually a kind of common denominator between the two approaches to urbanity represented by Lucilius and Terence, for on the one hand it shows clearly that the Roman is becoming aware of his superiority to non-Romans and other as yet non-Romanized outsiders, while on the other hand it stands for a Greek concept that has been brought to the city, examined, adopted, and integrated into urban thought as a thoroughly Roman phenomenon.

Before leaving Lucilius some mention must be made of the opinion of later writers that Lucilius was an *urbanus homo*. Cicero calls him cultured and very urbane (*doctus et perurbanus*), presumably referring to the cleverness and wit that he found in the *Satires*,[40] while in the *De Finibus* (1.7) he reinforces this opinion with the comment that Lucilius' poetry was colored by a remarkable wit (*urbanitas summa*) accompanied by only a moderate amount of formal learning (*doctrina mediocris*). Horace is also firmly convinced of Lucilius' refinement in the area of humor, though he too qualifies his praise.[41] It must be remembered that these two writers are using *urbanus* and *urbanitas* with contemporary connotations, since by the time of Cicero *urbanus* had evolved in meaning and application to where it stood for what was citified or urbane in manners, wit, and speech, and *urbanitas* had been adopted to describe this abstract urbanity. The conclusion that can be drawn from all of this is that Cicero and Horace could not find the aura of learning and the polished Latin style in Lucilius' poetry that characterized the literary products of their own times, but they did discover in him the kind of sophisticated wit which the urbane man of Rome strove to achieve. Herein lies one of the main reasons for Lucilius' continuing popularity among the ancients.

CHAPTER IV

THE CICERONIAN PERIOD

In contrast to the century and a half before 100 B.C., which was essentially a period of experimentation, the first fifty years of the first century are marked by careful analysis and precise definition. This makes the Ciceronian period especially important as far as refinement is concerned, since for the first time conscious attempts are being made to explain, interpret, and even define Roman urbanity. *Urbanus* occurs regularly now in extended meanings to refer to what is citified, sophisticated, or urbane, and *urbanitas* suddenly makes its appearance, perhaps coined by Cicero himself, to comprehend the wide variety of ingredients which were blended together in this Roman sophistication.

Just as the urbanite is now able to conceive of urbanity as something analyzable and definable, at least within general limits, so many of the feelings and attitudes stemming from it receive more frequent and more vocal expression. The opposition between city and country—what Cicero calls the *urbana expolitio* and the *res rusticae*[1]—and the Roman's awareness of the superiority of his way of life to that of Italian and foreigner alike are, if anything, more intense than ever before. In all of this there are overtones of an optimistic national pride, but there is also a solemn note, for every now and then Cicero hints that all is not well. The old Roman values are in danger and *urbanitas*, which is part of them, is threatened with pollution, dilution, and destruction from without.

Urbanitas AND THE *Urbanus Homo*

Almost every form of *urbanus* and its cognates now appears, whether it be adjective, adverb, or abstract noun, and there is such a wide variety of contexts that a semantic study produces rewarding results. But the natural tendency to catalogue and categorize these terms must be avoided, for just as sophistication and refinement do not lend themselves to a safe, sterile laboratory treatment, so the words that describe such attitudes and feelings cannot be treated in this way.[2] It has already been observed that by the time of Lucilius, while the adjective *urbanus* had not undergone any discernible extension in meaning away from the local, such a development was imminent. Early in the first century B.C. the Romans began to find new applications for the term and its cognates as the anonymous author of the *Rhetorica ad Herennium* shows when he boldly uses the double negative *non inurbanus* to convey the idea of polish and cleverness (4.51.64). This is certainly a semantic development that cannot be paralleled earlier, and yet the application and meaning are clearly anticipated by Plautus' use of *urbanus* modifying *scurra*, where the cleverness of a rather contemptible character is also under discussion and a similar note of irony prevails. The appearance of the abstract *urbanitas* in Cicero's *Pro Roscio Amerino* of 80 B.C. (120f.) argues for an awareness of a full-blown Roman urbanity at this time, for not only does Cicero use the noun without apology, but he assumes that his audience is completely familiar with it. Once again there is an aura of irony present, though it is attached to the whole passage rather than to the abstract alone.

Another writer who was aware of these developments was Catullus in whose poetry there is every indication that *urbanus* was connected almost routinely before 50 B.C. with urban refinement. In one of his more outspoken moods he gibes at Suffenus, and as he sets this character up for his epigrammatic fall, the poet repeats himself, calling him both charming, witty and urbane, and handsome and urbane.[3] Perhaps the adjective is synonymous with the words which accompany it as some believe, but this interpretation seems to dilute the meaning of these lines. In the first instance *urbanus* apparently extends the characterization from personal charm (*venustus*) and wit (*dicax*) toward cleverness and refinement, and these connotations remain a part of the meaning in the second occurrence where the adjective may be taken as neatly balancing the charming and handsome appearance (*bellus*) of Suffenus. Surely in these contexts *urbanus* is also meant to include the smartness, style, and good taste that marked the fashionable society of Rome, so that while there is an overlap with the words with which it is associated, it does carry important meaning of its own. Once again the sarcasm or irony that hovers about the word cannot be missed.

Although these are but a few of the examples that might be mentioned, they do serve to show that *urbanus* was associated with urban refinement soon after the turn of the century and that the Roman had come to accept this association as being perfectly normal—so normal, in fact, that he had created an abstract based on the adjective to refer to the phenomenon. When it came to describing this refinement, however, Romans like Cicero found that it tended to elude them. As he discusses figures of speech that are to be used by the orator, he mentions *odor urbanitatis* as an appropriate metaphor drawn from the senses (*De Or.* 3.161). Cicero is certainly correct in pointing to the obscurity and vagueness of the picture presented by this combination, for nothing is more difficult to describe than a fragrance, let alone a "fragrance of urbanity." In a passage of the *Brutus* (170f.), which will be discussed in detail a little later, Cicero all but admits defeat when he attempts to delineate and define the urbanity that marks the speech of a city-dweller. But if precise definition is not likely, the many scattered references to urbanity that appear in the literature of the time at least make description possible.

There are two conclusions to be drawn from the younger Cicero's suggestion to Tiro that since he has become a rustic, he should lay aside his urban ways (*urbanitates*).[4] In the first place, the city-country contrast is still very much in existence and a major point of difference is degree of refinement. Secondly, and more to the point for present purposes, the writer's use of the plural form shows that *urbanitas* is really a complex concept made up of a number of qualities, characteristics, attitudes, and the like. Marcus Tullius confirms this impression and also helps to narrow the scope of the term when in one letter he takes Trebatius to task for being unable to shrug off his "longing for the city and its urbanity," and then, reversing himself some months later, criticizes this same man in another letter for managing to escape these desires and for being "fickle as far as [his] craving for the city and its urbanity are concerned."[5]

The combination of *urbs* and *urbanitas* in these contexts seems to denote the surroundings and refinement of urban life and shows that while the physical attributes of the city are to be connected with *urbanitas*, they are not part of it. Cicero suggests the aura that pervades this urbanity when, writing to Atticus (7.2.3), he expresses a special delight with a certain Curius because of his αὐτόχθων . . . *urbanitas*. It is something innate in Romans, then, and it is predicated on a certain natural endowment. Cicero uses the Greek adjective to underline the exclusiveness of this phenomenon, and at the same time to relate *urbanitas* to the parallel concept in Athens, an allusion that certainly would not be wasted on Atticus.

In another letter, this one written to Curius himself, Cicero observes that this urbanity has been handed down from the past, that in his opinion it is undergoing a marked deterioration, and that its preservation is closely linked with the survival of the Republic.[6] In this instance there is only an implication that Curius exhibits this refinement, but it is worth noticing that Athens figures directly in the discussion.

Urbanitas, then, is an abstract idea—or perhaps it should be called an ideal—with many facets. It has been inherited from the Romans of earlier times and is a natural and integral feature of Roman life and thought. The passage of the *Pro Roscio Amerino* (120f.), in which the word appears for the first time, suggests itself as a place to begin a search for the components of this refinement. In this delightfully ironic episode the orator is denouncing Magnus and Chrysogonus for refusing to produce slaves for questioning, and as he does so he mentions literature twice, first pairing it with *urbanitas* and then with *humanitas*, thus implying that here the two abstracts have essentially the same meaning. *Urbanitas* remains a problem, however, since *humanitas* is another word which eludes definition. But the common denominator between the two seems to be good breeding and good manners, so that "culture" or "refinement" is probably the best equivalent for *urbanitas* here.[7] Its association with literature also suggests an alliance between urbanity and learning, although the fact that the two are separated hints that it may transcend the latter. Cicero leaves this impression once again when he admits that urbanity involves some knowledge of literature and the arts, but suggests that a sense of courtesy, a cleverness, a presence, and a charming wit are its real essence.[8] This, incidentally, is the clearest picture which Cicero gives of this Roman urbanity out of which comes that politeness that the urbane man is expected to exhibit at all times.[9]

Two of the most important outward manifestations of this refinement are a sophisticated humor and a careful manner of speaking which together set the urbane Roman off from those who are less refined both within and outside the city. By now *urbanus* and its cognates are regularly used relating to humor and wit. Not only does Cicero include among the necessary attributes of the orator "a certain charm of wit [*facetiae*] and a learning that is worthy of a free-born [gentleman]," but he insists that he should also have "a swiftness and brevity of reply and attack coupled with a grace, polish, and culture [*urbanitate*]."[10] The alliance between refinement and humor, then, is effected by *facetia* and *urbanitas* which together comprise the tasteful wit of the gentleman. Cicero may have this passage in mind later in this book of *De Oratore* when he asserts that *urbanitas* is the source from which the refined humor that pervades a speech should be drawn.[11]

In none of these comments is there any clear indication that Cicero is thinking of humor that is exclusively Roman, though the outlook of the writer and the purposes and circumstances of his writing make it likely that such feelings are not far away.[12] In other contexts, however, the overtones of a specifically Roman refinement are undoubtedly present. In a piece of flattery addressed to Paetus, Cicero speaks with respect of the Roman wits of olden time and expresses a delight in witticisms that are peculiar to the city.[13] Paetus is a brilliant ray of light out of the past because he exhibits this native Roman wit—noble, unsullied, and time-honored. The Romanness of what Cicero is talking about is to be seen not only in his mention of men like Lucilius and Laelius, but also in his observation that a foreignness is making its way into the city and is causing deterioration. The obvious parallel between *urbani sales* in this letter and the *sal et urbanitas* which Sulpicius uses in the *De Oratore* makes it a strong possibility that Sulpicius also had the city wit in mind.[14]

Mention of Lucilius in this letter to Paetus recalls Cicero's observation that the satirist's writings were marked by the highest degree of wittiness, though they did not always display a profound learning. The important implication here is that the capacity for urbane humor in the case of a man from the city was not necessarily contingent upon a thorough education. Cicero presumably considered life in Rome and association with refined Romans as being the most important contributing factors.[15]

There can be no precise answer to the question of what made this humor peculiarly Roman, simply because Cicero and his contemporaries do not describe it in so many words. It may be surmised, however, that, as with many other aspects of urbanity, it was as much the impression that it left as the actual content of a witty remark that marked it as being both sophisticated and Roman. This is in essence what Cicero means in the *De Officiis* (1.104) when he says: "Jesting takes two forms: there is the one kind that is low, insolent, shameful, and obscene, while the other is in good taste, refined (*urbanum*), clever, and generally witty (*facetum*)." In other words, proper wit is a faithful reflection of the manners and outlook that are expected of an urbane man of Rome.[16] With this comment Cicero has returned to the point he made in the *Pro Caelio* (6) regarding the contrariety of abuse and urbane wit, for in both cases insolence (*petulans, petulantius*) is opposed to cleverness and restraint (*facetus, urbanus, urbanitas*).

There is one element of the exclusively Roman humor that may be clearly identified. In a well-known passage of *De Oratore* (2.269f.), when Cicero turns to a discussion of irony, it is perfectly obvious from the narrative that the orator associates it with *urbanitas.* Not only do the words *lepus, perelegans,* and *facetiae* point in this direction, but Cicero also begins his discussion of irony by calling it urbane (*urbana*) and goes on to describe it as being particularly well suited both to formal oratory and to refined conversation (*urbanis sermonibus*).

Mention of refined conversation leads directly to the definition of an *urbanus homo* which is probably to be attributed to Valerius Cato, a contemporary of Cicero. While Cato's concept of urbane humor, as Quintilian points out,[17] is hardly perfect, he does recommend a broad application when he insists that the Roman gentleman must speak in a discreetly humorous way, no matter what the occasion may be—an informal conversation, a literary discussion with sophisticated friends, small talk at dinner table, or a formal public speech. The emphasis on *bons mots* throughout Cato's statement makes it obvious that he is not dealing with a general refinement in humor, but with the smart, witty, cleverly phrased, usually brief remark or rejoinder that was expected from the sophisticated man-about-town. This is the kind of cleverness that Catullus praises in Licinius[18] and the kind of repartee that passes between Cicero and Clodius in the courtroom.[19] It is certainly this aspect of Cato's account that makes the whole thing inadequate from Quintilian's point of view, for he cannot accept such a limited, un-Ciceronian interpretation. Even though the clever remark had its part to play in Cicero's and Quintilian's concepts of refined wit, *urbanitas* in their eyes went beyond the immediacy of repartee to flavor a man's whole speech. For them it was more of an aura which resulted from combining the up-to-date with the traditional, while for Cato *urbanitas* signified a smart, modern approach to humor which was no doubt better appreciated by the neoterics than anyone else.

The point has already been made more than once that a Roman's urbanity revealed itself in what he said and how he said it. Cicero makes a valiant, though rather unsuccessful, attempt to analyze this force of *urbanitas* in the *Brutus* as he discusses the merits of Italian orators.[20] In answer to a question of Brutus, he asserts that these "outside orators" have everything that is expected of a Roman speaker, except that "their speech is not, as it were, colored by a certain urbanity." Cicero's answer is extremely vague, and when Brutus presses him further for a definition of the term *urbanitas*, he is forced to admit that he does not really know what it is: "I just know that it is a certain [urbanity]." He then attempts a more positive approach by describing it as a more urbane sound and resonance that is heard in the voices of Roman orators.[21] But this too is obscure, for not only does a vague *quiddam* loom up again, but Cicero has defined the word in terms of itself (*urbanius*). The verbs he uses do indicate, however, that sound rather than style is under discussion.

After going on to mention that this urbanity marks the speech of many city-dwellers besides those indulging in formal oratory, Cicero at last resorts to examples. Tinca of Placentia in Cisalpine Gaul, for example, was bested by Quintus Granius "because of some kind of native flavoring [in his speech]." Mention of Granius immediately calls to mind the passage of the letter to Paetus in which Cicero includes Granius with Lucilius, Crassus, and Laelius as exhibiting the pure Roman wit. These two observations show that it is natural to view *urbanitas* as a unit, regardless of the fact that various facets of it may be singled out for discussion from time to time. From his final comment it is possible to see what this native flavor or *sapor vernaculus* is and to assume once again that sound is all-important: "Just as in Greece there is a sound that is characteristic [of the speech] of the Athenians, so among our speakers, as I see it, there is a certain sound [that marks the speech] of the urbanites."[22] The vagueness in Cicero's mind lasts to the end.

Crassus repeats much of what Cicero has said to Brutus when during his praise of Catulus' oratorical ability in the *De Oratore* (3.42 f.) he asserts that this orator's sound (*sonus*) and precision (*subtilitas*) please him. As he goes on to elaborate, he insists that he is not thinking of vocabulary but "a sweetness that comes from the mouth. Just as among the Greeks it is characteristic of the Athenians, so in the case of Latin [this sweetness] is peculiar to this city of ours." There are four obvious points of comparison to be made between this passage and Cicero's description of *urbanitas* in the *Brutus*, which when taken together suggest that the writer may have had these earlier observations in mind when he attempted his definition. In both cases vocabulary is carefully pushed to one side; sound as opposed to style is under discussion; the characteristic is peculiar to the speech of the man of Rome; there is a comparison between Roman and Athenian for essentially the same purpose. But Crassus is not finished, for he goes on to observe that just as even an uneducated man of Athens will easily surpass the "most learned Asiatics" in speaking, not so much because of the words he uses, but because of the sound of his voice, and not so much by speaking well as by speaking sweetly, so in the same way a Roman with little learning will have no trouble defeating a well-educated outsider such as Quintus Valerius of Sora "by the smoothness of his voice and by his careful pronunciation and vocal tone."[23]

It is perhaps presumptuous to pretend that this *urbanitas* which is so important a feature of Roman utterance can be defined with any more success or precision by us today than it was by Cicero who not only was in the position of a first hand observer, but was himself more sensitive to peculiarities of speech than most of his contemporaries.[24] And yet an examination of the terminology used in the passages already mentioned and in others where similar matters are being discussed is both interesting and informative. All of these words seem to be related to pronunciation and what might be called tone of voice or intonation. The *suavitas* which Crassus so admired in Catulus' speech sums up the *sonus* and *subtilitas* which appears to be a combination of a smooth intonation and a precise pronunciation that produced what would nowadays be called a cultured accent.

The *lenitas vocis* is also connected with tone of voice, for it is a mildness, gentleness, perhaps a smoothness of utterance. In view of the fact that Crassus contrasts this with a rustic harshness and a foreignness, it is entirely possible that it represents an avoidance of heavy, aspirated, guttural, and lisping sounds. The phrase *lenis appellatio litterarum*, which Cicero uses in the *Brutus* (259) to describe Catulus' way of speaking, apparently is meant to signify a careful pronunciation. That this pronunciation and tone of voice were related is to be gathered first of all from the occurrence of *lenis* here and secondly from the combination *oris pressus et sonus* which Crassus uses to designate the Roman way of speaking in the *De Oratore*. *Pressus* here is probably a precise and careful pronunciation, while *sonus*, as has been noted already, seems to apply to an over-all intonation. All of this adds up to what might be termed an urban accent. Just as nowadays the person who lives in a large urban center is marked as a city-dweller by a certain almost indefinable quality of speech, so apparently were the people who lived in ancient Rome. The phrase *urbanitatis color*, then, which the orator uses to describe this aspect of urban speech in the *Brutus*, is an excellent description of a phenomenon that is felt to pervade the utterance of a city-dweller, but which at the same time eludes description.[25]

Cicero's suggestion that this cultured accent is not to be acquired through formal learning has already been mentioned. He provides at least a partial answer to the question of what produces it in the *De Officiis* (1.133) when he says that if a certain natural endowment may be taken for granted, then subsequent practice (*exercitatio*) will increase clarity of voice, while imitation (*imitatio*) of those who speak with a careful pronunciation and a smoothness of voice will add to the sweetness of one's utterance. What Cicero seems to be getting at is the fact that a person can learn to speak clearly by taking lessons or by following some such regimen as Demosthenes did,[26] but that the sweetness of voice, which may equally well be called an urban intonation, is difficult to come by. People other than those born in the right circumstances could acquire it, not by sitting and studying, but by living in Rome and by associating with and imitating those who exhibited it. To put it another way, one had to become a Roman before he could have *urbanitas.*

This whole section of the *De Officiis* deserves closer attention, since matters of urbanity keep appearing. The point was made in the last chapter that Cicero was following Panaetius because he agreed with most of what the philosopher was saying and saw it as being directly applicable to Roman life and thought. It is also important to remember that Cicero was not simply translating but was adding ideas of his own and adapting the whole to Roman needs. In the passage already mentioned (1.133), for instance, not only is the vocabulary strikingly similar to that of the passages in the *De Oratore* and *Brutus* where *urbanitas* is being discussed, but a glance down the page immediately reveals a detailed treatment of the Catuli, at least one of whom was in Cicero's eyes an *urbanus homo*. This part of the passage, then, takes on a Ciceronian flavor and leaves little doubt that Roman refinement has its part to play.

The mention of the Catuli appears when Cicero is developing

Panaetius' views on the second or subordinate category of propriety which is made up of personal moderation and restraint accompanied by refined and gentlemanly action and appearance (96). In these paragraphs (96–140) a fairly complete picture of a gentleman and his qualifications is presented, with the topics ranging all the way from a man's appearance to the kind of home in which he lives. The way he stands, walks, sits, and reclines, his facial expression, the movement of his eyes and hands, all of these separately or together, must be neither effeminate nor boorish (128f.). Moreover, his masculine dress and healthful complexion combine to produce a neat outward appearance that is mandatory. His walk reinforces the impression of urbanity and so should be neither too lazy and slow nor too rushed. This is part of a more general feeling that the man of refinement should avoid becoming excited or harried for any reason at all (131).[27]

But it is on matters of speech that Cicero concentrates,[28] and this is the point at which the translator's personality and interests seem to predominate. In the first place, the ideal conversationalist must have a voice that is both clear and sweet. The second of these qualities has already been related to *urbanitas*, and here the speech of the Catuli is presented again as a good example of this sweetness which is produced by a careful pronunciation and a voice that is never strained, dull, inaudible, or, on the other hand, excessively melodious. The second aspect of polite conversation that Cicero stresses is a humor that always suits the occasion. There can be little doubt that the writer is thinking of urbane Roman wit, since he uses *sal et facetiae* as a designation and points to Caesar Vopiscus as a good example of one who was successful with it.

From here Cicero turns to present further attributes of the urbane conversationalist: he does not dominate the conversation; he suits the tone of what he is saying to the subject; he never shows a lapse in taste by talking of people not present to ridicule and insult them; he maintains the interest of his listeners by keeping to the topic under discussion and by limiting what he has to say;

he avoids irrational thoughts and activities and never shows anger, greed, sluggishness, or indolence; he always respects those with whom he is conversing; he seldom uses rebuke and then only when necessary and with restraint, making an attempt to criticize constructively; he never allows himself to boast. Most of this is just plain common sense, and there can be no doubt that the Latin faithfully reflects what Panaetius wrote, but the fact that the passage follows closely upon mention of the Catuli and Caesar suggests that Cicero sees a Roman application for these ideas. There can be little doubt that *urbanitas* and the *urbanus homo* are in his thoughts.

Aulus Gellius in his *Noctes Atticae* (13.11) shows that others were discussing such matters at Rome at this time when he reproduces Varro's description of a successful dinner party. Perhaps the most important part of the preparation involves inviting the right kind of guests, for they must not be too garrulous or too quiet and must be able to produce a conversation that is not excessively serious, but interesting and pleasant. If talk at table deals not with what is going on in high places in the Forum but with the experiences of everyday living that everyone has in common, then it will be charming and agreeable. Although Varro is speaking in a much more limited context than Cicero is in the *De Officiis,* he does put forward many of the same ideas and at the same time shows that he recognizes the same conditioning factor when he insists that strict rules of propriety be observed. If this is done, then the same results can be expected—a refined, urbane discussion in which everyone participates.

ROMAN ATTITUDES

The refined Roman was more outspoken than ever before in his refusal to accept those who did not exhibit or maintain the standards of urbanity that have been outlined above. In his eyes there were four groups who erred in matters of sophistication. First there was the man who had carried urbanity to an extreme and who for this reason might be called supersophisticated or hyper-urbane. Then there was the rustic who remained as before the stereotyped opposite of the urbane man. A third group consisted of the Italians living in the small towns who were not out-and-out rustics but belonged to the large middle class made up mainly of merchants and bureaucrats. Finally, the sophisticated Roman was becoming increasingly aware of differences between himself and non-Italian foreigners who were now migrating to the city in fair numbers.

THE HYPERURBANE MAN

In Ciceronian times when *urbanitas* was so highly valued and so carefully fostered, there must have been many in the city who pursued refinement to the point of overdoing it. It is remarkable, therefore, that mention of these people is relatively infrequent. The contempt that Cicero expresses for a Gabinius with his meticulously curled, well-greased hair[29] is a random comment that is not as detailed or as informative as one might wish. Much more helpful is the judgment that Cicero passes on Clodius and the remarks of Cicero and Catullus about one Gaius Arrius, both of whom went to extremes in matters of sophistication.

There were many reasons, of course, for Cicero's contemptuous treatment of Clodius, but his dislike was caused as much by the young man's habits, actions, and attitudes as by anything else. Clodius stands for the more permissive, smooth, up-to-date approach to life—*remisse, leniter,* and *urbane* are the words the orator uses—in which the traditional sophistication has little or no place.[30] It is no wonder, then, that Cicero cannot refrain from telling the court that this fellow is just too sophisticated (*urbanissimus*). In other contexts the orator's feelings about Clodius' softness and effeminacy are put more pointedly. At one point he calls him "a pretty little boy" and at another, after criticizing him for feeling that he alone knows what urbanity is, Cicero attacks his foppish ways.[31]

While Cicero singles out Clodius for special treatment, this young man is but one representative of a whole group in Rome for which the orator has little use. This is clear from the *Pro Caelio*, where Clodius and his sister are portrayed as the leaders of a smart, sophisticated set of "moderns"—young men- and women-about-town (67: *lauti iuvenes*)—who in their patterns of behavior show standards that a believer in the time-honored tradition of *urbanitas* cannot accept.

Cicero and Catullus combine talents to condemn one Gaius Arrius for what seems to be a hyper- or pseudourbanity. Cicero links him with a certain Sebosus and brands them both as hyper-sophisticates (*perurbani*). There is no doubt about how the writer feels, for he groans that he left Rome only to fall victim to these two creatures and tells how his first reaction was quite literally "to head for the hills."[32] He insists that he would rather consort with rustics than with such unpleasant characters. Cicero had already written to Atticus a few days earlier complaining that Arrius was a pest (2.14.2) who spent so much time on the doorstep that he was just like a roommate. But this is not the only problem, for this creature wants to sit around all day and philosophize, and though Cicero does not provide the details of this philosophastering, it is not difficult to imagine what went on.

Catullus presents another part of the picture in the delightfully humorous epigram in which he pokes fun at Arrius for an affectation in his speech.[33] This fellow not only aspirated the initial letters of words which needed no such embellishment, but even compounded his mistake by imagining that he was doing a "marvelous" job as he spouted his "*chommoda*" and "*hinsidiae*."[34] Catullus hints that this was a breach of urbanity when he uses *leniter* and *leviter* to characterize proper pronunciation, for these adverbs of lightness and smoothness may be linked directly to the smooth intonation and careful pronunciation that are part of *urbanitas* in speech. The picture of Cicero's being cornered by this character and having to listen to second-rate thoughts uttered with a condescending lisp is not without its humorous side.

Before leaving Clodius and Arrius, it should be pointed out that they represent two different kinds of hypersophistication. Clodius was aware of what *urbanitas* was, but simply chose to side with those who were reacting against tradition and setting up new, more extreme standards. Arrius, on the other hand, had no clear idea of what constituted urbanity, and so he made mistakes. He appears to have been a social climber who was trying to make himself out an *urbanus homo* in order to reach the right circles.

THE RUSTIC

Because in this period as before there are two kinds of existence, a city life and a country life, contrasting in obvious ways,[35] the urbanites and rustics are still routinely identified as two different groups[36] with two separate sets of qualifications.[37] The man of the city shows a remarkable interest in the rustic and his life at this time, and his attitude is not always one of opposition. But in matters of refinement the countryman is brushed off because he is basically ignorant and lacks polish.[38] Actually, he is still the same kind of character he has always been, wild and boorish, a product of a barren, rough, unsophisticated life,[39] all of which shows in his dirty appearance and the uncouth way in which he handles himself.[40] Moreover, he still exhibits the same simplicity and shyness that come from the fact that he spends most of his time in the isolation of the country away from the humanizing and refining influences of urban life.[41] As a matter of fact, in Ciceronian times, as in the time of Plautus, he is out of place in the city.[42] All of this is summed up in the adjectives *agrestis* and *rusticus* which continue as earlier to denote a general boorishness and lack of sophistication that may characterize a man whether he is a country-dweller or an unperceptive city-dweller. In addition, *rusticitas* is now coined, perhaps as a conscious antithesis to *urbanitas,* to indicate the sum of such characteristics.[43]

A number of explicit statements in the writings of this period shows more clearly than before how the refined man of Rome felt about the rustic. Because this life is still viewed as a kind of exile where the people live well-protected from the allurements and refinements of the city,[44] the man who lives in town can sneer at them for not having an interest in the same kinds of things that attract him. An extreme example of this attitude is Cicero's portrayal of the countrymen who follow Antony as being no better than cattle.[45]

But perhaps the most effective attack on boorishness is to be found in Catullus' clever treatment of Suffenus (22). This fellow is an urbane man and even somewhat of a man-about-town, so long as he does not attempt to write, but when he puts pen to paper he undergoes a complete transformation and becomes a mere ditch-digger and goatherd, coarser than the coarse countryside. Here Catullus has neatly balanced city and country to stress the contrast between the brightness of the gentleman which is revealed by his charming appearance, gracious manners, and effervescent wit and the dullness of the rustic which comes from a lack of any sense of propriety and an inability to articulate worthwhile ideas.

The urbane Roman was certainly conscious, then, of broad areas of incompatibility between himself and the rustic. But if he were asked to choose the one respect in which he felt this difference to be most conspicuous, he would probably select oral expression. Just as the urbanity of the city-dweller is revealed by what he says and how he says it, so the rusticity of a man from the farm shows itself as soon as he opens his mouth to speak. The urbanite recognized two ways of speaking Latin—one rustic and one urban.[46] Cicero contrasts the sweetness of utterance that is characteristic of the city with a rustic and boorish kind of speech which, incidentally, finds favor in some educated quarters. He repeats himself a little later, though he uses different words, when he insists that there is a manner of speaking peculiar to Rome which the Roman should cultivate in preference to a rustic harshness and a foreignness that arises from an inexperience with the language. The characteristics of rustic speech that make it harsh are briefly mentioned by Cicero when he goes on to describe Cotta's "rustic and boorish way of speaking" as a slow, heavy utterance marked by a rustic tone of voice. The words he uses to describe the impression left by this kind of speech are *aspere, vaste, rustice*, and *hiulce*.[47] *Aspere*, while it no doubt is meant to designate the over-all harshness of rustic utterance, refers in particular to a word arrangement in which too many consonants fall together. *Hiulce*, on the other hand, suggests what Wilkins calls a "disagreeable hiatus,"[48] while *vaste* seems to denote a certain flatness that pervades rustic speech.[49]

Of these characteristics, the last is the only one which Cicero elaborates when he says that the flatness of Cotta's utterance is at least partially due to his pronunciation of *i* as long *e*.[50] Varro offers corroboration on this point with the observation that people from the country say *veha* for *via* and *speca* for *spica*[51] and gives yet another example of this flat pronunciation when he points to the fact that the Sabine word *fedus* in the Latin countryside is *hedus*, but in the city is *aedus*.[52] Here there seems to be a balance between a rustic *hedus* and an *aedus* which would represent a more precise urban pronunciation.[53] Moreover, when Varro indicates that the flat version of *ae* was common among the Sabines, he may be pointing to an external influence on the speech of the *rustici Romani*. Varro alludes to this peculiarity once again in a later book of the *De Lingua Latina* (7.96), when he makes the incidental observation that the rustics pronounce *Maesius* as *Mesius*. His quotation of part of Lucilius' line on "Cecilius" as an example of the same phenomenon serves to underline the fact that this was nothing new.[54] It is also worth noticing that in *hedus* there seems to be a trace of an excessive aspiration that marked rustic speech. Confirmation is offered by Nigidius Figulus who asserts that "speech becomes rustic if you aspirate too much."[55]

As might be expected, Cicero was quite outspoken in his opposition to such rusticity, especially when it turned up in the city. By prefacing his remarks in the *De Oratore* with the eye- and ear-catching *Est autem vitium* Crassus—and so, by association, Cicero —leaves no doubt as to how he feels about Cotta's affecting rustic habits of speech. This coupled with Crassus' delight in Catulus' urbane speech reveals a Cicero who is defending *urbanitas* once again—this time from *rusticitas*. After praising Roman women in general and his mother-in-law Laelia in particular for preserving the old, pure *sermo Romanus,* Crassus returns to Cotta with a final condemnation: "And so our friend Cotta, it seems to me, is not emulating the orators of the good old days, but the reapers of the field." In Cicero's eyes, there is good reason for such a vigorous attack, for not only are many urbanites cultivating this rusticity, but the brighter ones are gaining good reputations. Cotta and Catulus are opposed once again in the *Brutus* (259) where the former is rather humorously pictured as traveling the "wild and heavily wooded trail" of rusticity to gain considerable respect as an orator. Regardless of what success he may have had, however, in the eyes of the experts he was merely an average orator.[56]

THE ITALIAN

Although the Italians are not clearly identified as a separate group, there is enough in what Cicero and his brother Quintus say to show that there was a small town element that could be isolated from both Romans and rustics.[57] The mixed feelings that the Romans had about these towns and the people living there stemmed from the fact that a majority of city-dwellers could trace their lineage back to one of these centers. At times these ties were so close that they presented problems of allegiance for the man who had moved to Rome.[58] At the same time, because the Italians were considered inferior, ridiculing another man's small-town background was an acceptable and effective way of insulting him in the law courts and Forum. Clodius, for instance, could ask Cicero why a boor and rustic from Arpinum was bothering himself with Baiae,[59] the implication presumably being that an Italian from a small town should not have any interest in such sophisticated pursuits. From this it would seem that if a Roman like Cicero maintained an allegiance to his town of origin, he could suffer such criticism, no matter how refined he might be. Again, it is interesting to notice that, while Antony insulted Octavian in a number of ways, it is his sneer at the future emperor for having a mother from Aricia that Cicero feels demands most attention.[60] The orator offers what appears to be the standard defense by suggesting the contributions that Aricia and towns like it have made to Roman life and by implying that Antony's lineage is not all that fine and noble, inasmuch as his father has a connection with Fregellae. And besides, other men like Philippus and Marcellus who have wives from Aricia are successful and perfectly happy.

Though Cicero defends the Italians with vigor and enthusiasm, he is still a man of Rome with an urban outlook. His attachment to Arpinum, for example, does not leave him blind to the fact that it is a rough and rustic part of Italy where entertainment is hardly the sophisticated variety found at Rome.[61] Nor is he above having a laugh at the activities of the town council of Pompeii.[62] But as in the case of the rustic, Cicero is most outspoken about matters of speech. As he comments on the capabilities of those orators living outside Rome,[63] he may be unwilling to call them foreigners, but at the same time he can find no generally accepted term to describe them. And so, adding a word of apology, he resorts to calling them "outside orators" (*externi*). Cicero mentions the Marsian Vettius Vettianus with his learned brevity and the brothers Valerii from Sora who were noted for their erudition, while Gaius Rusticelius of Bononia and Lucius Papirius of Fregellae are also names that Cicero feels stand out. The orator from outside the city who was the most eloquent of all, however, was Titus Betucius Barrus from the town of Asculum, several of whose orations were given at

Asculum, and at least one, an excellent speech against Caepio, at Rome. The note of respect that is present in what Cicero says about these *externi* comes not only from the fact of their being the best extra-Roman speakers, but also from the orator's feeling that he is one of them by virtue of his birth at Arpinum.

But it must be kept in mind that his main purpose in mentioning them here is to point up the fact that they do not have the cultured intonation and the careful pronunciation of the city-dweller. And so it happened that Titus Tinca of Placentia was bested by Quintus Granius, the Roman herald, in a contest of wit not because his efforts were any less humorous, but because Granius exhibited a certain "native flavor" in his way of speaking.[64] This was something that Tinca did not, and, for that matter, could not, have. In the *De Oratore* (3.43) Cicero passes similar judgment on one of the Valerii mentioned here when Crassus, after making the surprising statement that the Romans are less inclined to study literature than the Latins, points out that even the least learned of the urbanites can easily surpass Valerius. It is *urbanitas*—the combination of smoothness of speech, careful pronunciation, and right tone of voice—that makes this possible.

Cicero may have this criticism in mind when in another passage he briefly characterizes the Caepasii as having a small town way of speaking that sounds rough and confused.[65] This seems to be a fault that was opposite to the *urbanitas* of urban speech, but vocabulary that was unacceptable to the refined city-dweller may have contributed to the shortcomings of these orators. For even though Cicero is careful to omit diction from his discussion in the *Brutus,* he does admit that in Gaul, for instance, "you will hear certain words not current at Rome."[66]

THE FOREIGNER

As a large international center, Rome had long been paying the price of expansion in the cosmopolitanizing of her cultural and social life. Immigration from every corner of the Mediterranean was now at an all-time high, and perceptive Romans could see the effect that this influx was having on the city. In the eyes of Quintus Cicero, Rome had become "a city made up of a gathering of nations" and had developed into a breeding ground for intrigue, treachery, and vice of all kinds. The atmosphere created by the combination of prejudice, pride, hatred, and violence had produced stresses and strains that only the man of great foresight and versatility could avoid.[67]

Marcus Tullius complains of the situation in similarly strong language when he insists that so much scum has taken up residence in the city that there is nothing so low and vulgar that it does not appeal to someone. In his opinion the situation is extremely serious, for after asking his friend Volumnius not to let people foster coarse and crude sayings on him in his absence, Cicero sounds a plea: "Let us defend our claim to urbanity by whatever sanctions are necessary."[68] He puts it less dramatically in a letter to Paetus when he deplores the pejorative influence that the influx of foreigners is having in Rome. The fact that the traditional Roman humor has suffered from this "foreignness" (*peregrinitas*) raises a longing in Cicero for old-time wits like Granius, Lucilius, Crassus, and Laelius.[69] Though in both of these comments Cicero treats the influence only insofar as it involves the refined humor of Rome, there is no reason to believe that urbanity in general was not threatened. Indeed, the *peregrinitas* of the letter to Paetus is a force that might be expected to affect all facets of Roman life and sophistication.

The comments on the foreigner and his influence at this time disclose a consistently critical attitude on the part of the man of Rome. From Cicero's point of view Africans, Spaniards, and Gauls are repugnant wherever they are to be found, since they stand for everything that is gross and barbarous in humanity. People like the Scythians are even less acceptable. The Roman, on the other hand, is infinitely superior in any number of ways, and he never forgets it.[70] In fact, the most illustrious personage from a country like Gaul will come off second best in a comparison with even the lowliest Roman citizen.[71]

Catullus provides an example of what the Roman was trying to combat as he defended his *urbanitas* when, in two delightful pieces (37 and 39), he blackballs the Celtiberian Egnatius for being one of many who have infiltrated the city without being particularly successful in adopting urban manners. This "son of cave-filled Celtiberia," who is one of the long-haired foreigners frequenting the houses of ill repute in Rome, reveals his lack of urbanity not only in his appearance, but in the fact that he brushes his teeth with urine in true Celtiberian fashion. In the second poem Catullus describes him as perpetually smiling, even when the situation is a solemn one calling for tears. This habit is so deeply ingrained, so irritating, and so unnatural that Catullus calls it a sickness—a sickness that is characteristic of neither an elegant nor an urbane man. Throughout the two poems Catullus is a refined Roman talking to other refined Romans, in essence saying that this is the kind of person that Rome can do without.

Catullus may provide some idea of what the sophisticate in Rome was trying to combat, but, except for characteristics of speech, none of the traits which bothered the Romans receives extended treatment from other contemporary writers. In his comment on the influence that the influx of foreigners is having on Rome, Quintus Cicero makes the observation that a prospective consul must be well versed in the many different ways of speaking which he will encounter in the city.[72] The process by which this situation arose is outlined in the *Brutus* where Cicero asserts that all urban dwellers of earlier times who were not marked by an innate lack of sophistication spoke correctly, but that, as in the case of Athens, many people who speak a polluted Latin have gradually crowded together into Rome from many different parts of the world. The situation in Cicero's eyes has deteriorated to the point where the urbanite is going to have to take steps to purify and protect his utterance.[73]

74

Another look at the much cited passage of the *De Oratore* (3.44) shows that it is a foreign excess and strangeness which must be avoided by the urbane Roman if his speech is not to "sound or smell foreign." The vague terminology makes precise description of these shortcomings a problem, but there can be no doubt that vocabulary played its part. Sisenna's *sputatilica* formed on the analogy of the Greek κατάπτυστα suggests that the alien element was penetrating deeply.[74] But the kind of thing that Cicero is referring to here when he speaks of sound and smell is more likely reflected in his criticism of the poets of Corduba.[75] For to him they sound thick (*pingue*) and foreign, probably because their native tongue has exerted an influence on the way they speak Latin. The verb *sono* suggests that Cicero is thinking not so much of the written as of the oral word, and the vague *quiddam* shows that something more subtle than strange vocabulary is involved. The choice and ordering of Latin words contribute, but the slow, heavy sound is more likely a thick, foreign accent. *Pingue*, then, and *peregrinum* are to be taken as opposites of *presse*, *aequabiliter*, and *leniter* which Cicero uses to describe the urban accent.

In spite of his almost violent opposition to the foreign element in the city, Cicero has little to say by way of specific criticism of those Romans who exhibit *peregrinitas* in their speech. Even the rebuke offered to Sisenna for coining his horrendous word under foreign influence is relatively mild, and the disapproval is further mitigated by the observation that, though he was not the finest orator in the world, he was considered moderately successful.[76] Nor does the orator offer much detailed criticism of those who spoke Latin in the provinces. His feelings about the poets of Corduba have already been mentioned, so that it need only be pointed out here that he does not consider them worth a hearing and tries to discourage Romans like Quintus Metellus from promoting them. Again, while people of Narbonese Gaul must have had ample opportunity to learn Latin from the many Roman citizens who worked and traveled there,[77] the fact that Cicero includes a foreign manner of speaking among the constituents of the *peregrinitas* which was coming from that direction to threaten Rome suggests that the Latin which the native population spoke was not the best.[78] This is surely one of the reasons why Cicero and the other refined Romans of the time felt that Latin should be learned at Rome and not at some foreign center.[79]

Before leaving the urbanity and attitudes of the Ciceronian period it is necessary to emphasize the note of gloom and pessimism that turns up from time to time in Cicero's observations on *urbanitas.* The orator is obviously worried and depressed by the all-pervading foreign and rustic influences which he feels have inundated the city. So strong is his awareness of this presence that he insists urbanity is to be defended at any cost and urges remedial action. Cicero's pessimism comes from the reality of the threat, but it is reinforced by the fact that such influences are being accepted. Cotta, for instance, who purposely contrived a rustic accent, has achieved a good reputation as an orator, and Romans of good family like Metellus have welcomed the help of second-rate foreign poets like those from Corduba.

But there is a second reason for Cicero's gloom. As he writes to Curius he utters a desperate plea: "Do come, then, please, so that the seed of *urbanitas* does not die along with the Republic."[80] This letter was written in 44 B.C. when the disintegration of the Republican traditions was well under way. Since for Cicero *urbanitas* is one of these, it is no wonder that he is at once defensive, militant, and pessimistic regarding it. But it is wrong to do as some have done and take Cicero's words as meaning that *urbanitas* was in a decline,[81] instead of recognizing the fact that such comments are part of his generally pessimistic view of life at the end of the Republic. The fact of the matter is that *urbanitas* did not disappear in 44 B.C., even though the Republic did.

CHAPTER V

THE AUGUSTAN AGE

HORACE AND *Urbanitas*

Almost every aspect of the life and literature of the Augustan Age shows some influence of sophistication. A mere mention of the literary circles of a Maecenas or a Messalla conjures up a picture of peace, quiet, and refined leisure, though some of those who directed artistic endeavor at this time, Maecenas and Agrippa, for example, seem not to have been as urbane as one might expect.[1] Even a quick glance at the evidence shows that in this period urbanity is approached from two quite different points of view. On the one side is Horace who reveals himself in his poetry as a product of the traditional *urbanitas*, while on the other there is Ovid who promotes a new and modern kind of refinement which he calls *cultus*.

Because it is easy to talk in a general way about Horace as an *urbanus homo* by pointing to the exquisite poetry of the *Odes* and the philosophic restraint of the *Satires* and *Epistles*, most references to his refinement have been broad statements which treat *urbanitas* as an indefinable and almost mystical quality that pervades his writings.[2] But it is perhaps fairer to Horace and at the same time more enlightening to avoid such generalities and try to take into account what he has to say about *urbanitas* and how it manifests itself in specific instances in his poems.

Once again there is no clear definition and no detailed discussion of the concept. Perhaps the most general pronouncement that the poet makes is to be found in the introductory remarks of the *Epistle to Lollius* (1.18.1–20) where the idea seems to lie behind what is being said, in spite of the fact that words of urbanity do not appear. The whole poem, which has been described as "a lecture on court etiquette,"[3] is an account of how the golden mean is to be employed in dealing with a patron. There are two extremes that must be avoided if a person is to recommend himself as a true friend, one of which is represented by the *scurra* who is fawning and servile and so quick to agree with the patron, almost repeating him verbatim, and the other by the rough rustic with his shaved head and black teeth, who is always ill at ease and always ready to wrangle about something or other, no matter how trivial it may be. Horace does not name the "virtue" that lies between, but the more one ponders, the clearer it becomes that *urbanitas* is at least part of it.

There is a striking similarity between Horace's comments here and what Aristotle says at two points in the *Nicomachean Ethics*. In one of these passages (4.1126b.6.1–4) the philosopher presents an antithesis involving obsequious, flattering people on the one hand, who praise everything and never offer any kind of objection, and grim, quarrelsome individuals on the other, who are negative on principle and never worry about irritating or hurting people. The man of good sense, who lies between these extremes, approves and disapproves as the situation demands, all the time adjusting his manners and attitudes to the rank of the person with whom he is dealing and taking care not to give offense. The overtones of urbanity in this description cannot be missed,[4] though Aristotle does not attempt to name the man who falls between the toady and the boor.

In the second passage, where the topic is still propriety in action and outlook, Aristotle turns to wit (4.1128a.8.3) and speaks of buffoons who go too far with their joking and boors who have no sense of humor at all. In this case the man who falls between these extremes is the clever wit (εὐτράπελος) who shows good taste and tact at all times.

The parallels between what Aristotle and Horace are saying are obvious not only in the balance and the mention of friendship, but in the fact that Aristotle's clever wit is echoed in Horace's Eutrapelus who makes his appearance a few lines later (31).[5] The parallelism suggests a direct connection and shows that *urbanitas* is the virtue that lies between Horace's *scurra* and *rusticus*. But the first few lines of this poem should not be read in isolation from the rest, and when the connection is made it becomes clear that *urbanitas* in Horace's mind is part of the golden mean—a sensitive, sophisticated approach to relations with other men.

This urbanity is at least tacitly connected once again with a happy moderation when Horace indulges in criticism of various people's habits.[6] Maltinus, for example, represents one extreme in fashion as he lets his toga all but trail on the ground, while another elegant soul (*facetus*) wears his so short that his buttocks nearly show. Similarly Rufillus who has perfume on his breath is balanced by Gargonius who smells like a goat.[7] In both contexts matters of refinement are surely under discussion, and it is strongly implied that true urbanity lies between the extremes that are being described. But it would be wrong to conclude that Horace puts great emphasis on externals, for elsewhere he insists that while people may laugh at a man because his hair is cut in rather rustic fashion, because his toga drags on the ground, or because his shoes flop and scuff, there may exist beneath this unsophisticated exterior a good and noble man, a good friend, and a great genius.[8] The mention of rusticity and friendship recalls the *Epistle to Lollius* where *urbanitas* and friendship are somehow related, and the two passages together imply that, while rusticity and urbanity may involve externals, it is a man's actions and thoughts that reveal this true *urbanitas*. The fact that Horace has to speak so explicitly here and elsewhere[9] about the unimportance of externals suggests that there was in Rome at this time a strict set of rules for sophisticated dress and behavior.

Horace's use of *urbanus* in his poetry tends to confirm what has already been said. As he speaks against backbiting and gossipy wit in one of his *Satires,* he rises to a sort of climax with mention of the dinner guest who begins his evening's activity by joking at the expense of everyone except his host, but soon "sprays" him also. "If," Horace says, "this person seems to you genially and wittily outspoken (*comis et urbanus liberque*), do I seem to you spiteful and backbiting (*lividus et mordax*) just because I laugh at a Rufillus and a Gargonius?" (1.4.86–93). With the ironic application of the adjectives here Horace is really branding the toady as a backbiter, while the poet himself becomes witty by comparison. Urbane wit, then, is still very much a part of *urbanitas* and, as before, subtlety, good taste, and propriety are the essence of it.[10]

By far the most important and informative references to refined humor come from contexts in which Horace is treating literary matters. It is both interesting and at the same time surprising to note, for instance, that ideas about Plautus have changed. While earlier generations praised the playwright's wit,[11] the present generation has developed a more sophisticated outlook in such matters and has learned to differentiate between the inurbane and the tasteful witticism. The earlier people mentioned here must go back beyond Cicero, but they probably include him, for he had coupled Plautus with the writers of Old Comedy and Plato and had described them as exhibiting the kind of speaking that was elegant, urbane, clever, and witty.[12] A passage in one of Horace's *Satires* (1.10.9–19) suggests the basis for his criticism of Plautus. Satiric style is to include matter that is both serious and witty with the former coming from the sober utterance of the rhetorician and poet and the latter from the urbanely humorous man. The true wit takes great care not to overstate his case, and he does this by sketching a fine and subtle humor usually marked by a brevity of style. Although Horace does not make the point in so many words, it would appear that Plautus' boisterous, brawling early Roman humor lacks this subtlety and restraint that the poet connects with *urbanitas*.

This does not mean, of course, that there is no urbanity in Plautus' plays. It does indicate, however, that concepts have changed. Horace's views on the subject are conditioned by the fact that he sees an evolutionary process at work in Roman literature where the primary function of the Augustan poet is one of pruning and refining. This is evident from what Horace says in his *Epistle to Florus* where, as he outlines the poet's role, he uses a metaphor from rustic life in which the roughness of earlier poetry and that of rustic life are combined in the adjective *aspera*, while Roman refinement and cultivation of the fields appear as *cultus* (2.2.122–25). The evolutionary activity which Horace describes here appears in more explicit detail in the well-known lines of the *Epistle to Augustus* (2.1.139–270), where the poet describes an evolution in Roman literature resulting from a kind of tension between rusticity and urbanity in which the latter gradually prevails. As far as Horace is concerned, Plautus comes too early in the scheme. Lucilius, on the other hand, represents a later, though by no means final, stage inasmuch as his poetry reveals a partial urbanity. He is genial and urbane in matters of wit, but he does not write in the economical style of Augustan times.[13]

Not only are there suggestions and reflections of urbanity on almost every page of Horace's poetry, but in many cases the poems themselves are clearly manifestations of the poet's *urbanitas*. This is especially true of the *Satires* where even the title *Sermones* is meant to recall the polite conversation that the Roman gentleman cultivated so carefully.

A few examples from the *Satires* and *Epistles* stand out as being worth special consideration. Though it is placed with the *Satires*, the poem in which Horace describes his journey to Brundisium (1.5) is hardly a satire at all. It is more of an *urbanus sermo*, a monologue tastefully put together by a refined narrator, in which other urbane men like Fonteius Capito, who is "a gentlemen to the tips of his toes," as well as Plotius, Varius, and Vergil, "the fairest of souls," keep making their appearance. But the urbanity of the poem is better seen from the impression that it makes on the reader. Cicero would say that there is an *odor urbanitatis* about it which comes from an all-pervasive wit that is at the same time quiet, good-natured, and ironic.

It is possible to overlook the adjective *ignavus* towards the beginning (5) in which the poet cleverly and ironically smiles at his own shortcomings and creates a light mood that is repeated in his declaration of war on his stomach (7ff.) and in vivid pictures (11–23) of the lazy mule and the sophisticate's discomforts ("those damned flies!"). The mock-heroic description of the encounter between the two lowlifes, Sarmentus and Cicirrus (51–69), represents a situation that verges on the burlesque, but the treatment is lightly and carefully done. The mock epic tone of this episode is repeated in the potentially slapstick picture of the burning house at Beneventum (71–76). Throughout this poem the humor is accompanied by a gentle irony that reveals the writer as "a witty, urbane man carefully conserving his strength."

There are two other poems of Horace that deserve even closer attention—the *Epistle to Claudius* on behalf of Septimius (1.9) and the satire in which Horace encounters a persistent bore (1.9). The letter to Claudius almost speaks for itself, since it fairly exudes refinement and tact. Horace informs his correspondent that he has agreed to speak on Septimius' behalf since it would have been ungracious, unrefined, even boorish of him to refuse in the face of the other's persistent requests. The poet is emphasizing his own urbanity here, but as he does so he is careful not to make too much of Septimius' requests so that Claudius may not consider the other man tactless. When Horace goes on to say he has resorted to the privilege of "urban frankness," he is not only cleverly emphasizing the fact that he is behaving as an *urbanus homo*, but is also indicating that the whole letter is a piece of *urbanitas*. The request which follows is simple and frank, flattering no one: "Enter this fellow in the number of your flock and believe him a good, stout-hearted man." In all probability there was a smile on Horace's lips as he penned the word *gregis* in the last line, for this rustic touch neatly contrasts with and so underlines the urbanity of his request. There is just a hint of a subtle and urbane wit at work.

The well-known satire in which Horace describes the miseries of meeting a persistent parasite in downtown Rome (1.9) is actually a rather interesting study of an *urbanus homo* in what was probably not too unusual a predicament. Horace's good manners are undergoing a severe test from a person who in his whining, wheedling, and fawning ways resembles a *scurra*, but who also exhibits a blatantly boorish attitude to life. The poem is a humorous study of various attempts on the part of the gentleman to get away from this pushy and generally detestable character.

As the action unfolds, the victim tries to cope with the situation in his own way by remaining aloof and by trying to brush off his opponent politely but firmly. When the fellow keeps persisting, Horace becomes more and more desperate, but his natural politeness and restraint never desert him. He varies his gait, makes up a story about a sick friend across the Tiber, suggests that the boor leave him when he is torn between staying and going to court, and grasps at Aristius Fuscus, another *urbanus homo*, as a *deus ex machina*. At no time does Horace express his true feelings, though the irony that lies behind some of his answers and observations would have been easily understood and quickly acted upon by someone more sophisticated than the bore.

This satire is particularly interesting because the reader is taken into the mind of the gentleman and shown the torment that exists there. The point is clearly made that outward propriety does not always reveal inward thoughts, and often disguises them. By showing the workings of his mind, the poet is better able to smile at the gentleman for failing to cope with the realities of an existence where inurbanity prevails.

Horace, then, is perfectly well aware of *urbanitas* and its influence, and proves himself in his poetry to be an urbane man of the times. In the satire just mentioned the reader has no doubt as to how Horace feels about his gauche and unsophisticated opponent. Such attitudes find expression elsewhere in his poetry. While the few derogatory comments he makes about foreigners and Italians either represent commonplaces or stem as much from other feelings as from any sense of exclusiveness and refinement,[14] the poet's views on the country are both interesting and important. There is no need to dwell on his admiration and idealization of the country life, except as these ideas relate directly to feelings of urbanity, but it is worth pointing out that in a number of instances he uses the simple and peaceful life of the country as a foil for the urban affluence and the trials and tribulations it brings.[15]

This contrast is elaborated in the famous satire in defense of country life (2.6) where it becomes increasingly clear as he makes his case that Horace is not advocating any retreat from refinement. He is simply recommending the rustic peace, quiet, and simplicity without visualizing any violent change in the manners and outlook of the person attaining it.[16] The *sermo* he recounts (70–117) bears this out, for Cervius' story of the city and country mice is a delightful blending of *rusticitas* and *urbanitas*. It is rustic, inasmuch as it is a simple allegory filled with moralizing in mono- and bisyllabic words. But the cleverness and the urbane wit that run through the story keep the reader aware of the gentleman who is writing the poem. The rustic Cervius here is the same kind of character as Ofellus in an earlier satire (2.2) who has been called a rustic Socrates.[17] Both have risen above the proverbial rustic ignorance.

The poet's praise of the country which he directs at Aristius Fuscus[18] shows another dimension of the city-dweller's attitude to rustic life. Fuscus, who incidentally is the one who left Horace at the mercy of the bore, is a sophisticated man of Rome who is described at the beginning of this poem as a lover of the city. It is clear from what Horace says that he is one of those gentlemen who are unable to leave Rome under any circumstances. Not only does he have this close attachment to the city, but he has a strong antipathy towards the country and all it stands for. This is a different kind of outlook from that of Horace who can fully appreciate things rustic but is not for that reason any less refined. It is important to notice that Fuscus is treated as a close and respected friend by the poet and that there is no implication that he is wallowing in the sensual luxury of the city.[19]

Horace, then, is one of a group of refined Romans who, while not advocating a return to rusticity, have a full appreciation of what the country can mean to a man from the city in terms of relief, respite, and leisure. This outlook, of course, is not far different from that of Xenophon or Cicero who had earlier exhibited a similar appreciation of the rustic scene. But like them Horace also realizes that there is a wide gulf between city life and country life. His account of Volteius who was duped by Philippus into becoming a man of the country clearly shows this.[20] Though this character entered wholeheartedly into the metamorphosis, even to the point of adopting a shaggy, unkempt appearance, everything went wrong for him and he was soon back begging Philippus to restore him to his former state. It is dangerous to press all of this too far, for though Volteius is described as being *nitidus*, Horace carefully points out that this man is an auctioneer living in modest circumstances. The fact remains, however, that the poet recognizes the impossibility of an urbanite's becoming a true rustic.

Horace is as aware as his predecessors had been of the roughness, ignorance, and general boorishness of rustic people. When he speaks in the *Ars Poetica* (212f.) about the ignorant rustic hobnobing with the city-dweller, "the lowly with the well-born," there is a realistic, almost cynical note that betrays the outlook of the urban gentleman. Elsewhere Horace laughs at the rusticity and boorishness of the bumpkin, surely by now proverbial, who stands waiting for a stream to pass so he can cross[21] and smiles in the direction of the countryman as he warns his messenger not to carry his books awkwardly under his arm as a rustic carries a lamb.[22] Lucullus' soldier from down on the farm may show a shrewdness in replying negatively to his general's exhortations, but the reason this is noteworthy is that some form of ignorant answer was expected of him.[23] Part of the idealized picture of Ofellus the rustic is a rough, homespun kind of philosophy,[24] and, even though he turns out to be a "rustic Socrates," the implication is strong that the average countryman cannot be expected to show deep and subtle thinking. The vile language that Rupilius Rex spouts should also be mentioned here, for it comes from the vineyards of Praeneste and is characteristic of the rough, tough vine-dressers thereabouts.[25]

The point has already been made that Horace's feelings about rusticity are an important part of his view of the evolution of Latin literature.[26] In his eyes literary activity in the broadest sense of the term had its beginnings in a city that was rustic and consisted at first of the merrymaking of the early farmers which soon produced the rustic insults of the Fescennines.[27] Here is the basic roughness, the *rusticitas,* with which the poet eventually had to cope, though before his appearance it was mitigated in content, at any rate, under threat of law. Another restraining and refining influence came from the direction of Greece, who "took captive her captor and brought the arts into rustic Latium." The plural *artes* stands out as revealing Horace's recognition not only of the great influence of Greece on Latin literature but also of her effect on Roman refinement in general. In spite of this pressure, the Roman *rusticitas* continued to make itself felt, so that traces of rusticity (*vestigia ruris*) remained even in Augustan times. One of the main reasons for its persistence was the unwillingness on the part of Roman poets to prune and refine.[28] Rusticity, then, as it must be avoided in other facets of the urban and urbane life, must not be allowed to appear in formal literature. Horace, the *urbanus homo,* has spoken.

OVID AND *Cultus*

Born in 43 B.C., Ovid represents the younger generation of the Augustan Age for whom the upheaval that Horace and Vergil had witnessed at first hand had little reality. By the time he began to write, the *Pax Augusta*, which for the older poets represented a goal towards which the civilized world had been striving for many years, had come to be a normal state of affairs, and the long cherished *otium* was now taken for granted and even showed signs of developing into the notorious *desidia* of the next century. In Ovid's case this atmosphere of peace, quiet, and leisure was reinforced by a personal *otium* which enabled him, in spite of a father's wishes to the contrary, to follow his own poetic interests.

His background, his personality, and his genius combined to make sophistication the very essence of Ovid's poetry. It has been said with good reason that he teaches "*cultus* of the person" as Vergil had taught "*cultus* of the fields."[29] Refinement so pervades his writings that, except perhaps in the *Metamorphoses*, it seems to be the *raison d'être* for most of them. Perhaps it is not going too far to say that the poet's sense of sophistication overpowers and for the most part replaces any depth of thought that might otherwise have been expected from his poetry.

Because of this commitment on Ovid's part, there is a strong antithesis between him and the poets of the older generation like Vergil and Horace. Higham has summarized the contrast rather well: ". . . Ovid and his opponents lived on different planes and could find no common ground for argument. His standards were aesthetic, not moral."[30] Wilkinson puts it a little differently when he describes the *Ars Amatoria* as "the reaction of a witty and high-spirited member of a sophisticated circle to a puritanical and sometimes hypocritical orthodoxy backed by power."[31]

It is no wonder, then, that the urbanity of Ovid's poems leaves quite a different impression from that which is found in the writings of Cicero and Horace. A striking indication of this difference is the fact that, while Ovid has an intense interest in refinement and urbanity, he nowhere uses *urbanus* to refer to it. In fact, the word occurs only three times and then only in a colorless, locative sense.[32] Apparently, this word and its cognates connoted a traditional view of urbanity that the poet could not accept.

A survey of Ovid's writings reveals that, while each in its own way is an important reflection of his culture and sophistication, there are three that stand out as being particularly informative. As a study of both male and female urbanity the *Ars Amatoria* is unique, for here all the rules for sophisticated behavior are laid out clearly and relatively concisely against a background of urbane wit. On the other hand, the *Tristia* and the *Epistulae ex Ponto* are almost as important, since they provide clear insights into what happens to an *urbanus homo* when he is taken out of his sophisticated society and given complete and thorough exposure to all that is inurbane.

In a well-known passage of the *Ars Amatoria* (3.101–28) Ovid talks about refinement in some detail. His subject in this book is the process of cultivation (*cultus*) which a woman must undergo in order to make herself attractive to the opposite sex, and in these lines the poet indicates that this is part of a larger refinement (*cultus*) that sets his times off from earlier times. Though in the old days there existed only a rough simplicity (*simplicitas rudis*), Rome has by now become a golden city, as a glance at the magnificent Capitol, the stately senate house, and the Palatine with its fine dwellings will show. Ovid revels in the present: "Let old-time things please others," he says, "I thank god that I was born now and only now." It is important to notice that as the poet speaks he is careful to dissociate himself and his desires completely from the contemporary pursuit of wealth and luxury, for it is too easy to ignore his assertion that he is not interested in gold and all it brings (124–27) and to link him with the opulence and prodigality of the wealthy. He goes on to say that this age is well suited to his makeup because culture, refinement, sophistication, urbanity which can all be summed up in the one word *cultus* are everywhere (127). But Ovid does not stop here, for not only is he convinced of the omnipresence of *cultus*, but he is also quite certain that rusticity, which in his mind is its diametrical opposite, no longer exists in contemporary Rome. Here he disagrees with Horace, of course, who felt that traces of *rusticitas* remained in Augustan Rome.

The writer leaves no doubt, then, as to how he feels. He is a modern, sophisticated man reveling in the refinement of the city, and when he expresses his dislike of the good old days he is in essence pointing to the fact that he cannot be a Horace or a Vergil who can reconcile present and past. It may have been a feeling that these poets and people like them were somewhat hypocritical and a little too pious in uttering such sentiments that led Ovid to observe elsewhere, "We praise the ancients, but we enjoy our own times."[33] However this may be, the importance of what he says in the *Ars* cannot be overemphasized, for in these lines the universal *cultus* appears—*cultus* of the fields, *cultus* of the person, *cultus* of the intellect, and *cultus* in the broad sense of Roman refinement—all put together in an evolutionary context.[34]

A search for manifestations of this refinement shows the first and most obvious to be Ovid's poetry itself. Because he asserts that he is writing "cultivated poems" which take their place beside other worthy poetry of the time,[35] a poem like the *Ars* may be viewed as "an aspect of Roman civilization, of the new culture that had finally overcome the rude simplicity (*simplicitas rudis*), the rigid morality and the rustic naïveté (*rusticitas*) of his ancestors."[36] At the beginning of the *Medicamina Faciei* (1–28), in a passage remarkably similar to that from the *Ars* discussed above, Ovid in essence says that *cultus* has inspired this little poem, and after elaborating a contrast between the old, rough Sabine ways and the modern sophistication, he makes his point concisely and precisely: "Our times have elegant gentlemen" (24). Here too there is a similar feeling that cultivation of the land provides proof of what *cultus* in general can achieve and that civilization and its refinement have undergone an evolution that is almost complete. This is a theme that is developed in the *Metamorphoses* where the fact that *cultus* in one form or another occurs some thirteen times suggests that refinement and sophistication were very much on Ovid's mind as he wrote.

These examples are enough to show that his poems are designed, as Higham says, "to add a refined pleasure to life," and that in them there is "a poet . . . striving to acclimatise in Rome a kind of poetry that required his own liberal sympathies and cultivated taste for its appreciation."[37] As a matter of fact, Ovid's talent and inspiration were so bound to this sophistication which had Rome as its focal point that once he was exiled from the city he was unable to continue writing in the same vein.

The *Ars Amatoria* is the first extended treatment of sophistication that has been preserved, and, while the emphasis is on male behavior, it takes on a special importance from the fact that female refinement receives careful treatment. Ovid would begin with a student who has some awareness of what is involved, while rejecting outright unperceptive outsiders such as those who come from the barbarian Caucasus (3.195–200). In this way he feels he can create a woman that is worthy of a lover, one that he can call "the most accomplished and sophisticated lady possible" (1.97).

From here Ovid proceeds to touch upon just about every aspect of the appearance and manners of the ideally sophisticated woman, at the same time stressing the importance of decorum in each instance. A show of luxury, for example, must be avoided when it comes to choosing and wearing jewelry (3.129–32) or clothes (169–92). A lady's hair should be arranged stylishly to complement the face,[38] and her clothes must be carefully suited to her person in color and type (3.169–92, 267–70). Mannerisms are also to be watched carefully, since everyone has physical shortcomings which should not be broadcast (3.261–80). There is, for example, a decorous and demure way to smile, while openmouthed belly-laughs and tearful laughter must be avoided (281–88). When it comes to walking, a lady is expected to show a feminine grace (3.298), avoiding the swaying body and pointed toes of the hypersophisticate and the long, lumbering steps which characterize the rustic (3.299–306). Here is a clear contrast between *cultus* with its implied propriety and the two opposite extremes of hyperurbanity and *rusticitas*.

This propriety extends also to the way the sophisticated lady handles her emotions, for under no circumstances is she to give way to angry outbursts or to any show of pride, arrogance, or gloom, but she must leave the impression at all times of being a happy, well-adjusted person (3.237–42, 499–524). She should also show a versatility which includes singing, playing the lyre, reading poetry, dancing, and playing women's games (3.315–80). Finally, her refinement must reveal itself in the Latin she speaks and writes.[39] All of this adds up to Ovid's *cultissima puella*, and though it would be possible to spend much more time ferreting out the details of her appearance and character, this is enough to suggest a picture of the poet's poised and sophisticated woman-about-town.

Because Ovid's main interest in his amatory poetry lay with the young lady as a desirable object of pursuit, he is not as precise about the qualifications of the urbane young man who is her pursuer. The information that Ovid does convey, however, is certainly important to an understanding of his concept of urbanity. The poet recommends that the gentleman be immaculate without going to extremes, that is, without becoming a hypersophisticated dandy[40] with curled hair and well-scraped legs. The touch of neglect that Ovid describes as being desirable here is not to be interpreted as involving even a trace of rusticity, for the poet goes on to say that a man must be clean and healthy-looking with polished nails, shining teeth, spotless toga, well-fitting shoes, neatly-cut hair and beard, pleasant breath, and no bodily odor (1.513–22). Accompanying this careful grooming are accomplishments in the arts and in both languages (2.121f.), for the refined young man is expected to dance and sing, if he has the talent (1.595f.), and to write verses and recite them with a compelling charm (2.283f.).

The manners of the *homo cultus* reflect a sense of propriety and consideration at all times, especially in his attention to his lady's needs (1.149–62) and in his compliments to her (1.619–30, 2.281–86). Above all, the young gentleman avoids roughness and harshness (2.145f.: *asperitas*), whether it be in taking kisses (1.663–72), in avoiding quarrels (2.151f.), especially those leading to physical harm (2.169–74), in pressing his suit (2.529f.), or in offering criticism (2.641f.). Under no circumstances are force and pushiness to be used, since the key to a successful relationship between the gentleman and his sophisticated lady friend is peace (2.175f.). Even these brief comments on male urbanity in the *Ars Amatoria* reveal that the gentleman observes a code of manners which is not unlike that to which the lady is bound.

Ovid's treatment of *cultus* in the third book of the *Ars Amatoria* shows that the poet has no use for the past and its *rusticitas*, and his many other comments on the rustics and their rusticity reinforce this impression. But before examining in detail what he says about *rusticitas*, something must be said about his more positive pronouncements on rustic life. As the poet begins to describe and praise *cultus* in the *Ars*, he relates "cultivation" to a country context in order to show its universal importance. The positive approach here is repeated in the *Fasti* (1.663–704) where Ovid gives an outline of the ritual and prayer that will, among other things, ensure successful tillage (678: *cultus*), keep birds from harming the plants under cultivation (683: *cultis*), and prevent the sterile wild oats from growing in the carefully tilled soil (692: *culto . . . solo*). There may be a trace of the pastoral and an appreciation of the country and its ritual in these lines, but, except for the "crowned heifer" (663) and the "warm springtime" (664), idealizing elements are missing, and Ovid maintains an interest that is surprisingly academic.

There is a certain feeling, however, that gradually impinges itself on the reader as he makes his way through these lines. This is best described as a note of impending doom and an atmosphere of gloom stemming from an awareness of all the difficulties that threaten the farmer (680–92). While this pessimistic tone continues in the theme of ploughshares being beaten into swords (697–700), the poem does end on a positive note with thanks to the gods and Augustus for the peace that has brought the farmer back to his fields. Perhaps this passage may be described as showing Ovid's feeling for country life,[41] so long as this does not imply a purely positive outlook, for the poet knows full well that rustic life is difficult and that ritual is necessary to overcome at least some of its problems.

The same didactic atmosphere pervades the well-known passage in the *Remedia Amoris* (169–98) where Ovid suggests that getting away to the country and involving oneself in rustic activities will help to cure the pangs of love. Here he tends to idealize the country as a place of retreat and a source of restorative power for the city-dweller in much the same way as Horace had, for the field is described as giving back with interest the seeds that have been sown (173f.), trees are shown bending under the weight of the fruit (175f.) as brooks flow babbling along (177), and the shepherd sits nearby playing his tune on his pipes (181). Fall gives fruits, summer grain, spring flowers, and even winter has something to offer in its crackling fire (187f.). If the distraught lover will become a rustic and throw himself into this kind of life, he will find an enjoyment and a distraction in it (193f.), so that "as soon as this joy begins to soothe your [troubled] mind, Love loses his effect and leaves on feebly flapping wings" (197f.).

There may be a "full and genuine enthusiasm" for the country here, and the description may be "fine enough to challenge anything written on the subject by other Roman poets,"[42] but there is a difference between the way Ovid develops his picture and the way in which Horace expresses his delight in the country. Because he is producing a cure for love, Ovid's interest is once again basically academic. This is why his account sounds like a list of ingredients for a prescription, and this is the reason for his recommending that the lover take his medicine only until he is cured. Not only is there no implication that he will stay in the country, but the poet fully expects him to return to the city when he is well.[43] It is worth noticing that Ovid does not appear in this country scene at all. Nowhere does he enter the picture as Horace does to show that these are experiences that he has had and enjoyed, but he remains the physician who can prescribe a medicine and describe what it will do for the patient, though he has never taken it himself.

Ovid the doctor has indeed been speaking a few lines earlier where, significantly enough, he speaks in his own person for the first time in this part of the *Remedia:* "People may call my advice hard and cruel. Yes, I admit it's cruel, but you'll have to put up with a lot to get your health back."[44] These words, which are meant to apply both to the prescription for travel which immediately precedes them and to the prescription for country living which follows them, are extremely important, for they show clearly that for the *homo cultus* being away from urban life and its sophistication is a serious hardship. This is not Horace's reaction at all.

At first sight Ovid's romantic picture of the countryside around Sulmo in the *Amores* (2.16.1–10) may appear to have much in common with this passage from the *Remedia*, but the fact that it is an intensely personal passage makes it quite different. Ovid's attachment to the country comes through better here than anywhere else in his writings, for in a few lines he puts the reader in the fields of the Paeligni and soothes him with cool streams, pleasant breezes, green grass, and luxuriant crops and vines. The only part of the ideal rustic atmosphere that is missing is the shepherd piping a tune in the shade of a tree while his flock grazes nearby. But this addition would be impossible, for it represents the ultimate in leisure and quiet, and it is clear from the lines following immediately upon this introduction that Ovid feels anything but peaceful in his situation. After an intervening lament over the pangs of frustrated love, the poet relates himself to this ideal country life (33–38) by mentioning a few of the activities in which

94

he cannot bring himself to take part and by pointing to the fact that he cannot enjoy the cool waters and refreshing breezes. In these lines of the *Amores*, then, the picture is one of perfection, and Ovid himself is the central figure.

Artistically, the poem is a delight, for the peaceful country presents a clear contrast to the seething feelings of the inner Ovid and the alternation between the two reflects the wide-ranging emotion of the lover. Perhaps it is art for art's sake, since with Ovid one can never be certain. But if the poem is taken at face value, it is possible to read into it an intense and honest attachment to the country which is quite Horatian, in spite of the fact that Horace professes to find complete release in the country, while Ovid is unable to do so.

Before leaving this poem from the *Amores*, we must note the inconsistency that exists between it and the advice given in the *Remedia*. There the poet suggests that retreat to the country will solve the lover's problems, while here in the *Amores* Ovid shows that such a prescription is ineffectual. One wonders whether the poet remembered his *Amores* as he wrote the *Remedia*.

Though it is different in matters of detail, there is a similarly romantic view of the country in the *Tristia* (3.12.5–16). It is cold in Tomis and as consolation Ovid conjures up a picture, not without a certain yearning, of the happy return of spring to the Italian countryside. The poet apparently has no particular place in Italy in mind as he imagines the boys and girls frolicking about picking the flowers that bloom in many-colored profusion in the fields. The swallow, surrounded by other chirping birds, is busy building her nest; the grain and vines are beginning to sprout and the trees are beginning to bud. Though this is a delightful picture full of Ovid's longing for Italy, the lines which follow (17–26) help to put it in the proper perspective. Here Ovid the gentleman, suddenly shifting his attention from the country to the city with its fora, city festivals, games, and theatres, rises to a climax with a note of longing in his voice: "Blessed is he who is allowed to enjoy the city at will." *Urbs* is the key word here, and it is this, not the country, that Ovid really misses. He is an urbanite with urban thoughts, so that, even though he may have a feeling for country life,[45] his love for the city remains foremost in this thoughts.[46]

In a second epistle from exile there is another very personal account of the countryside around Sulmo not unlike that which he has painted in the *Amores*.[47] Here the poet's longing reveals itself in his description of the gardens on the pine-covered hills and in his reminiscences about his past farming activities which are evidenced still by the trees planted by his own hand. Then, in a framework of "If only I had a plot there," he presents Ovid the goatherd, Ovid the ploughman, and Ovid the farmer doing his sowing, weeding, and irrigating. This is an effective picture in which there is much of Ovid's love for the life around Sulmo. But if it is to be fully appreciated, the whole context must once again be taken into consideration.

Ovid begins this letter to Severus by coupling the many miseries he is experiencing at Tomis with a brief history of the city (1–24) and then suddenly becomes emotionally incoherent, first protesting that he really does not long for the pleasures of life at Rome (*urbanae commoda vitae*) but then almost immediately reversing himself. As it turns out, these are precisely what he wants,[48] since he proceeds to list the people and things that he misses: his friends, his wife, his home, "the places of the beautiful city," the fora, temples, marbled theatres, the porticoes, the Campus, the gardens, the pools, and the aqueduct Virgo (29–38). At this point Ovid states unambiguously where he stands as far as city and country are concerned: "But I imagine that if I must be miserable and not able to enjoy the city, I may at least take some pleasure in the country."[49] There follows the picture of Sulmo and Ovid the ideal rustic, which has already been discussed. Then, returning in his mind's eye to the city (65–70), the poet with envy and longing pictures Severus now in the Campus, now in a shady portico, now, though rarely, in the Forum, and soon strikes a fresh note as he visualizes his friend going off to his Umbrian or Alban estate. Here once again Ovid, as always, returns to the urban and the urbane. Perhaps he can appreciate the peace, quiet, and restorative power of the rustic life and he may be able to think fondly back to his childhood at Sulmo, but because he is the victim of his sophistication, he can never view the country impartially.

It has already been noticed that in his pronouncement on *cultus* in the *Ars Amatoria* the poet refers to a rough simplicity and a rusticity associated with earlier times which he rejects in favor of contemporary sophistication. The kind of rustic roughness to which he is referring is exemplified in the *Metamorphoses* (14.519–23) by the shepherd who is changed into a wild olive tree after spouting out "rustic insults laced with obscenities." Though the context may be completely mythological, the combination of *improbat* and *convicia rustica* recalls the *opprobria rustica* which Horace saw as the rustic beginnings of Latin literature.[50] The theme of *rusticitas* and the past is elaborated briefly in the *Medicamina Faciei* (11 f.) where the coarse Sabine woman of Tatius' era is contrasted with the gentler and more genteel maidens of Ovid's time.[51]

As might be expected, this roughness and boorishness is portrayed most often as something opposed to cultured, sophisticated life. It may take the form of a boorish hesitancy, for example, that can cause a girl problems in fulfilling her love.[52] In another context Ovid insists that it is not any sense of restraint and shame that keeps a man from enjoying complete success once he has managed the kisses, but a boorish ineptness which has no place in such matters.[53]

The letters exchanged by Helen and Paris in the *Heroides* (16 and 17) are worth examining in this connection, since the theme of *rusticitas* keeps appearing among the thoughts expressed. Background is provided by the lines in the *Ars Amatoria* (2.365–72) where Ovid says quite frankly that Menelaus was stupid to go off and leave his wife alone with Paris who was by no means a rustic guest. Indeed, as he writes to Helen this sophisticated lover speaks contemptuously of the boorish Menelaus and his love-making (*Her.* 16.221 f.); he has already told Helen that as a woman born in rural Therapnae she is in no position to refuse him simply because he is a Phrygian (195f.). In answer to his charge that it is a boorish simplicity that prevents her from yielding to him in love (16.287f.), Helen admits to her rusticity, especially as far as a man like Paris is concerned, but says that she is willing to remain in this state, if it means that she will not forget her sense of decency (*pudor*) and will maintain a faultless life (17.11–14). It is not long, however, until she changes her mind and convinces herself that she should give in to Paris. But even at this point she does not know what to do, for she feels that somehow Paris should use force to drive her *rusticitas* from her (175–88) but cannot imagine how the process will work.

The change that she has undergone by the end of the letter is really quite remarkable, for not only has she become the sophisticated young lady of the *Ars Amatoria*, but she has even left her door ajar for her lover. As far as Menelaus is concerned, the situation is hopeless, for not only was he foolish to leave Helen behind in the same house with Paris, but he has no room for complaint even if he should find out what is going on, since "the fellow who lets the fact that his wife is having an affair bother him is just plain boorish and doesn't know the ways of the city."[54] Here the relationship between love and rusticity is perfectly clear, for *amor* is one of "the ways of the city" that add up to *cultus* while *rusticitas* represents a failure to appreciate this refinement.[55]

Not only does Ovid express himself on the relationship between urbanity and rusticity, but he also passes judgment on foreign barbarity. His poems from exile reveal in almost intimate detail the influence that a barbarous and uncivilized people could have on a man of refinement.[56] It must have been a terrible experience for a gentleman so attached to Rome and its sophistication to be plunged to the opposite extreme at the end of the world. Time and time again the poet who was so articulate about matters of refinement shows himself to be at a loss as to how to cope with the barbarous creatures at Tomis in whom he can find no trace of civilization.[57]

His ideals of sophistication are so completely overwhelmed that he even contemplates death when he considers the habits, dress, and language of these people.[58] The poet who wrote of the sophisticated lover with his spotless toga, neatly trimmed hair and beard, and impeccable manners is surrounded by barbarians with savage sounding voices and wild looking countenances whose untrimmed hair and beard and animal skins and breeches make them look more like wild creatures than human beings.[59]

Intellectual stimulation is nonexistent at Tomis, for the arts have not yet reached the end of the world. Ovid's sophisticated poetry demands a refined audience, but there is no one except the barbarian to hear him.[60] From this it is easy to see how dependent the poet had been on his fellow sophisticates in Rome. But a bad situation is made even worse by the fact that Ovid knows of no one who even understands Greek and Latin, though some Greek heavily flavored by the uncouth sounds of Getic has apparently managed to survive.[61] Ovid, then, is forced to learn the Getic and Sarmatian languages,[62] and there is something pathetic about the pride he expresses at having become competent in them and in his boast that here among the savage Getae he has an incipient reputation as a poet.[63]

The poet complains that what poetry he is managing to write is being affected by this barbarity, so that he is no longer to be compared with Roman poets.[64] "If by some chance," he says, "my poems seem not to be written in Latin, it is because they were composed in a barbarian land." Ovid suggests that at least one area affected is vocabulary,[65] but the fact that his poetry from exile does not show such influence suggests that it may all be a stance. If it is, it is the stance of an urbane Roman, for Ovid is consistent in calling his "little books" from exile foreign and unsophisticated and pointing to the fact that their motives for being in the city should be questioned.[66]

It is because sophistication and sophisticated poetry as he knows them cannot exist outside Rome that Ovid cries out from exile in longing for his friends in the city and for all the places which remind him of his refined life there. Nor is it surprising that he is prepared, as a second choice, to settle for a life in rural Italy. At times he may merely want someone with whom he can speak Latin, but what he really needs is a sophisticated friend to comment on his verses.[67] He writes to Atticus in reminiscence of the kind of thing he misses—the delightful chats, both serious and full of wit, Atticus' appraisals of his poems, the walks and experiences that they enjoyed together in downtown Rome, all tempered by a mutual affection.[68] Ovid ends this poem with a request: "Do defend your old companion as far as you may—just so long as I don't become a burden for you." Not only does the gentleman cling to memories of sophisticated friends and activities, but he also continues to mind his manners.[69]

Ovid's letters from exile supply further insight, then, into the makeup of the *homo cultus.* These poems come as much from his sophistication and his clear knowledge of what it is as do the *Ars Amatoria* and his other poems of love. In the *Amores* and *Ars* the poet revels in his refinement, while here he struggles to maintain his sanity in an atmosphere that is in every way completely antithetical to what he has grown to appreciate. Augustus chose Ovid's place of exile with care. For such a man as this it must have been a living hell.

THE *De Urbanitate* OF DOMITIUS MARSUS

It has already been suggested that by Augustan times *urbanus* and *urbanitas* were regularly employed not only to designate a Roman sophistication as it appeared in humor, but also to denote urbane wit itself. Horace was not the only Augustan writer who was aware of this application of the terms. According to the elder Seneca, Asilius Sabinus was a very witty person (*urbanissimus homo*) who compensated for his lack of eloquence with an urbanity of wit (*urbanitate*).[70] Seneca also expressed the opinion that the younger Cicero had inherited nothing from his father except an *urbanitas*, which, in spite of the context, would appear to be a refined, well-developed sense of humor.[71] In each case the abstract noun may have the overtones of Roman exclusiveness that originally clustered about it, but an unbiased appraisal of these statements leaves the impression that it, like *urbanus*, has taken on the more general connotations of refined wit.

Two examples of Sabinus' humor follow closely upon the mention of his *urbanitas*,[72] the first revolving around a clever play on customs, and the second depending on a play on words. After being asked by the people of Crete to take up their highest magistracy, Sabinus, fully aware that traditionally the Cretans holding office let their hair and beard grow, cleverly remarks that he has already twice held this office in Rome. He is referring to the fact that he had been a defendant in court, where it was customary for the accused not to trim his hair and beard. This is an extremely clever witticism, so clever, in fact, that not only did the Greeks not understand it, but Seneca has to explain it for his readers. The second example is a little less abstruse, since the point of this humorous remark lies in Sabinus' reference to one Turdus (Thrush), who is a thoroughly despicable character, as a "dainty dish." It is hardly what one would call great wit, but it is both clever and pointed.[73]

While these two witticisms reveal a strong Roman flavor, two instances in the *Suasoriae* within a few lines of one another (1.5) show that *urbanitas* is now not only taking on more general connotations, but is being used more concretely. In the first instance the urbanity consists of a clever quote from Homer's *Iliad* (5.340) by an unnamed philosopher as he contemplates the wounded Alexander. This wit expresses his wonder that blood is flowing from the general's wound and not "ichor such as flows in the bodies of the blessed gods," since, after all, Alexander considered himself a god. The general used his sword to pay the philosopher for this bit of wit (*urbanitas*). The joke itself is clever enough, but what is significant in this passage is the fact that the abstract noun has come to stand for the product of urbane wit, the clever remark, an application that will become common in authors of the next generation. A little later in the same context *urbanitas* is used once again without any particularly Roman overtones, this time to refer to a clever and ironically humorous comment of Cicero. Here, however, the emphasis seems to be on the abstract idea of wit rather than on the concrete witticism.

It is a pity that Domitius Marsus' treatise on *urbanitas* has not survived, not only because of the light it would shed on urbane humor, but also because it seems to have contained much in the way of literary criticism. At least this is the impression one gets from the scant but tantalizing information offered by Quintilian.[74] Since it is impossible to know for certain what the exact title of the treatise was, it is perhaps safest to assume that Quintilian has preserved at least the essence of it when he says that Marsus "wrote very scrupulously *de urbanitate*."[75]

The writer seems to have begun with a definition of *urbanitas* and followed this with discussion and elaboration which contained, among other things, Valerius Cato's definition of an *urbanus homo*. When the connection between *urbanitas* and *urbana dicta* had been established here, the latter were then apparently analyzed under appropriate headings and subheadings with illustrative material drawn from earlier writings.

As far as the subject of the treatise is concerned, it is obvious that refined wit must have played a prominent part, since Quintilian asserts that the theme was not laughter in general, but *urbanitas* (103). Marsus' definition which Quintilian quotes in the next paragraph helps to clarify the meaning of the abstract: "*Urbanitas* is a certain force (*virtus quaedam*) compressed into a brief saying that is effective in charming men and moving them to every emotion. It is especially well suited to defense or attack depending on which the situation and the opponent demands." The lack of precision in what Marsus says is quite striking, and the combination *virtus quaedam* immediately calls to mind Cicero's similarly vague treatment of *urbanitas* in the *Brutus*.

There is also a comparison to be made with Cato's definition where the same emphasis on *dicta* is found and where the same conditions of proper and universal application prevail. Just as Cato's *urbanus homo* was characterized by *multa bene dicta responsaque*, so, according to Marsus, *urbanitas* is a certain quality contained in short sayings (*in breve dictum coacta*). Cato's insistence that his *urbanus homo* speak humorously and decorously (*commodeque*) and Marsus' assertion that *urbanitas* is suitable to defense or attack as circumstances demand both suggest that a sense of propriety is fundamental to their separate conceptions. But within these similarities there is a basic point of difference, for the universal application of *urbanitas* in Cato's definition consists in the urbane man's being ready to speak wittily under any circumstances, while for Marsus it means that he is able to arouse any emotion in a man. To put it a little differently, Cato is clearly interested in the man who will never fail to raise laughter (*risus*), while Marsus is interested in *urbanitas* which will raise the complete range of emotions. It was perhaps an awareness of this difference that caused Quintilian to preface his remarks with the statement that Marsus was not writing about *risus*. It is also possible that Marsus included Cato's definition in his discussion with a view to criticizing it on this point.

Quintilian's account of the *urbana dicta* in the *De Urbanitate* tends to confirm what has been said and at the same time gives clearer insights into the nature of this *urbanitas*. The sayings which contain urbanity may be serious (*seria*), humorous (*iocosa*), or intermediate (*media*). The witty utterances would in all likelihood be those expected of Cato's *urbanus homo*—clever remarks tastefully chosen to raise a laugh, which were surely well enough known that they needed little discussion by Quintilian. He feels it necessary, however, to discuss the *urbana dicta seria* which he says are subdivided by Marsus into complimentary (*honorifica*), insulting (*contumeliosa*), and intermediate (*media*). From the examples Quintilian provides it is also obvious that these *dicta* are brief, clever, pithy, and well phrased.

The more closely they are scrutinized, the more evident it becomes that they are strikingly similar to the usually terse, well-phrased expressions called *sententiae* which were carefully cultivated and used so effectively by the better orators. There is neither the time nor the space to discuss these at any length here,[76] but the line from the letter to Atticus which Quintilian quotes as an example of a serious *dictum* that is insulting (8.7.2) provides a direct connection between the two. He quotes it again (8.5.18) during his discussion of modern trends in the use of *sententiae* where it serves as an example of a pithy statement which depends on an element of surprise for its effect (8.5.15). To be specific, it is a *sententia* which achieves the desired result through a balance of opposites (*ex contrariis*). Its sententious purpose cannot be missed when it is viewed in context, for after suggesting that Pompey has rendered his case all but hopeless, Cicero neatly and cleverly puts a sting in the tail of this part of the letter by asserting that he has now someone to flee—that is, Caesar—but no one to follow.

Although he does not include the examples of the complimentary and intermediate *dicta* that are drawn from the *Pro Ligario* and the *Catilinarians* in his discussion of the *sententiae*, these can easily be assigned to Quintilian's categories. The pithy remark from the *Pro Ligario* naturally falls with those pronouncements that achieve their effect by surprise, and in the context it serves not only as a subtle expression of Cicero's view that Caesar should pardon the defendant, but it summarizes and points up what the orator has been saying about the good and bad that Caesar has experienced at the hands of the Ligarii.

The example from the *Fourth Catilinarian* is a little different, for it is a *sententia,* inasmuch as it is brief, clever, and well expressed and because it is used by Cicero to give point to what he has been saying to the senators about looking out for themselves and the government, but, at the same time, because it is less personal, it can be lifted out of context and used as a maxim. If Quintilian were labeling it, he would most certainly call it gnomic or aphoristic (8.5.3).

It is now time to return to the question of what it is that Domitius is discussing in his *De Urbanitate.* It has already been noticed that he calls *urbanitas* a certain *virtus* which he finds in *dicta,* so that if there is a close relationship between *dicta* and *sententiae* as has already been suggested, it would be natural to imagine that *sententiae* too have this certain intangible something. Surely the most important abstract quality that is common to all of the examples of *dicta* and *sententiae* that Quintilian mentions is something that might be called "point." Perhaps, then, *urbanitas* may be described as the power inherent in a concise expression to summarize, underline, and illustrate by catching the attention of the reader or listener through nicety of thought and expression. If this is true, then the *De Urbanitate* seems to have been a well-organized and exhaustive study of that rather elusive literary quality which for want of better terminology may be called "sententious point."

That Marsus should be interested in pithy remarks and the "point" contained in them is perfectly logical, since he was an epigrammatist, and it is the brief, clever concluding remark, usually referred to as the "sting in the tail" or the "point," that sets the epigram off from all other literary forms. Just as it was natural for Cicero to give orations and write treatises on the nature of oratory, so it would be nothing out of the ordinary for Domitius to produce epigram and at the same time analyze its essential characteristics in a study such as the *De Urbanitate.*

The choice of *urbanitas* to refer to epigrammatic point, whether made by Marsus or not, is a particularly happy one. In the first place, it is a word of refinement and culture which can also signify the cleverness and the wittiness of the well-bred Roman. The examples chosen by Marsus and the *sententiae* quoted by Quintilian all exude sophistication, cleverness, and in most cases a subtle wit. But even more important is the fact that *urbanitas* still has strong overtones of Romanness, so that when Domitus uses the word it should convey something of purely Roman flavor to the reader. The "point" that he is discussing, then, takes on Roman overtones, and with this realization comes the recognition of the basic difference between *sententiae* and Marsus' *urbana dicta*. The former are not exclusively Roman.[77]

A search beyond the *sententiae* for the "point peculiarly Roman" leads right back to the Roman literary epigram, since the pointed epigram of a Marsus or a Martial, while it was ultimately derived from Greek lyric poetry, was considered a Roman development in which the evolution of the type lay mainly in the gradually increasing emphasis on the pithy remark that concluded the poem.[78] The *De Urbanitate*, then, was apparently an analysis of the most significant characteristic of Roman epigram. While this application of *urbanitas* is new and different, there is really no other label that could be given to this literary quality and characteristic that would be as appropriate.

LIVY'S *Patavinitas*

Unfortunately, not as much is known about views on correct speech in the Augustan period as might be wished, for there is no Cicero who talks at length about the subtleties of the urbane accent, pronunciation, and diction. It is possible to read some information into scattered passages from major authors such as Ovid and Horace, but for the most part it is random allusion in one or two of the less important writers of the period that provides what evidence there is.

When Nepos points to the outstanding sweetness of the voice

and utterance of Atticus,[79] he seems to be referring to the same combination of vocal qualities which connoted *urbanitas* in speech for Cicero. A little later this same writer describes Atticus as having a sweetness in his Latin speech that produced a certain charm that was innate and not something that left the impression of having been acquired.[80] With these words the Ciceronian *urbanitas* comes to mind once again, for not only do these comments recall Cicero's references to the harmonious sound of Catulus' voice which made speech particularly Roman,[81] but they also remind the reader of Cicero's discussion of *urbanitas* in the *Brutus* where he qualifies his observations in much the same way and defines his quality as an innate flavor (*sapor vernaculus*) of speech. In fact, the similarities are so striking that it is tempting to see a Ciceronian influence on the terminology of this passage. However this may be, Nepos represents a bridge by which the interest in urbane speech moved from the Ciceronian period into the Augustan Age. That the interest continued after Nepos is shown by Seneca's description of Cassius Severus' manner of speaking where the writer suggests that what stands out for him is the orator's sweetness of voice which results in a pleasant, forceful-sounding utterance.[82]

Attitudes to and comments on the inurbane also suggest that the Romans of this period were as aware of *urbanitas* in speech as their predecessors. Seneca's qualification of Catius Crispus as a provincial orator,[83] in which there is a certain note of superiority, calls to mind Cicero's discussion of Italian orators in the *Brutus*, though in this case it is Catius' affected, clumsy, bombastic way of expressing himself that comes in for criticism and nothing quite so subtle as an inurbane accent.

More important is what Seneca says about Porcius Latro,[84] for after giving a vivid picture of the man and his habits and after mentioning that he had a strong voice which suffered because he never exercised it, he asserts that Latro's main problem was an inability to shake off his rough, rustic Spanish habits which did not provide the regimen needed for care and cultivation of his oral expression. In other words, he was unable to take on the Roman refinement so necessary for complete success in oratory and declamation. Latro's Spanish origin must have been evident when he spoke, for Messalla, who was "a most conscientious guardian of Latin speech,"[85] when he heard Latro declaiming could not resist commenting that he was "eloquent in his own peculiar language." Messalla was apparently quite ready to grant intelligence to the man, but could not tolerate his habits of speech. It would be idle to speculate on the details of Latro's shortcomings, since Seneca does not elaborate. It is enough to notice that Ciceronian feelings in matters of speech were still very much in evidence and that knowledgeable littérateurs such as Messalla were still the outspoken guardians of *urbanitas.*

Messalla was not the only Roman of his time that was aware of urbanity and inurbanity in speech and Latro was not the only Spaniard that came in for this kind of criticism. Seneca quotes Cicero's description of the poets of Corduba by way of characterizing the speech of Sextilius Ena, a Spaniard with more genius than polish.[86] It has already been suggested that Cicero was criticizing a thick foreign accent that was evident when these poets opened their mouths to speak or recite. If it can be assumed that Seneca used the description in the same spirit and with the same meaning as Cicero had, then it is at least a logical assumption that his criticism came from a similar awareness of the careful accent and tone of voice of the urbane Roman.

There is a bothersome point that must be raised, even though there seems to be no explanation of the difficulties it presents. In the passage just mentioned Seneca goes on to recount an anecdote in which Ena is portrayed as reciting at Messalla's house with Messalla himself present. If the host is really a "conscientious guardian of Latin speech," then it is difficult to see how he could even abide such an inurbane speaker as Ena, let alone sponsor a reading by him. There may be political and social pressures at work that can no longer be discovered.

Finally there is Pollio's well known criticism of Livy's *Patavinitas* which is mentioned twice by Quintilian.[87] In the later and more important of the two passages the author is discussing *elocutio* or oratorical delivery and style with the express purpose of showing how in the broadest sense words should have nothing foreign and non-Roman about them. In particular, he is advising against speech which shows an excessive precision, rather than a relaxed Latin idiom. The kind of thing he is talking about is illustrated in the Greek by Theophrastus' use of a single word which, because it was too precisely Attic, indicated to the old woman who heard him that he was a foreigner. By way of offering an example from the Latin side Quintilian says: "and besides Asinius Pollio thinks there is in Titus Livy, a man of great eloquence, a certain *Patavinitas*." He then goes on to observe that all words and utterance should smack of Rome so that one's speech may seem clearly Roman and not something given with citizenship.

The adjective of uncertainty that is used to qualify the abstract reminds the reader of the doubts that Cicero had about *urbanitas* in his attempt at a definition in the *Brutus*. Another point of comparison lies in the fact that the anecdote about Theophrastus occurs in both places. The impression the rhetorician leaves, then, is that Pollio was discussing a characteristic of speech opposed to *urbanitas* for which he coined the word *Patavinitas*. Moreover, the combination *verba omnia et vox* suggests that both dialect and accent are included, so that it may be more precisely correct to consider *Patavinitas* the opposite of *Latinitas* and *urbanitas* together.[88]

The second passage in which Quintilian makes mention of Pollio's criticism (1.5.55f.) more or less confirms what has already been said, although here it is vocabulary alone that is under discussion. Overtones of *urbanitas* appear once again in the mention of Lucilius' criticism of Vettius which was earlier related to the developing Roman urbanity of the second century B.C.

It is difficult to be more precise about what is being criticized, since, as has been pointed out often enough, any attempt to present an analysis of Livy's Patavinity is doomed to failure simply because Pollio's statement covered details and subtleties that even for Quintilian were no longer identifiable. Some years ago the suggestion was made that this Patavinity lay in Livy's pronunciation and accent and that this shortcoming was related to that exhibited by Tinca of Placentia who was chosen by Cicero as an example of a provincial orator lacking the mysterious quality of *urbanitas* in his utterance.[89] A glance at a list of the dialectal peculiarities of the Latin of northern Italy that may have colored the speech of Tinca and Livy reveals two that are already familiar as being characteristic of speech that is rustic and so inurbane. These are an apparently flat pronunciation of the diphthong *ae* as long *e*[90] and improper use of the aspirate, at least from an urbanite's point of view.[91] The occurrence of a flat pronunciation may be borne out by Quintilian's observation that Asconius and Livy both used the forms *sibe* and *quase* for *sibi* and *quasi*.[92] Throughout this section the writer seems to be dealing with the written rather than the spoken word, though he says in another connection that spelling and pronunciation may coincide.[93] But even if these alternate forms are drawn from Livy's *History*, it is interesting to speculate that they may represent the influence of the historian's flat pronunciation on his writing. That this flatness is peculiar to the Latin of Patavium itself is suggested by the fact that both Asconius and Livy came from that center.[94]

It is perhaps best to stop at this point, for insurmountable problems stand in the way of further explication of *Patavinitas*. Not only is the context of Pollio's observation unknown, but Quintilian, who quotes it, is himself well removed from the atmosphere of the Augustan Age and cannot know what influences from contemporary literary attitudes and what hints of personal and political irritations lie behind the remark.[95] The importance of Pollio's criticism is simply that it shows a continuing awareness of *urbanitas* which makes it impossible for the Roman gentleman to accept anything provincial.

CHAPTER VI

THE FIRST CENTURY
AFTER CHRIST

Perhaps the most significant development in this century as far as urbanity is concerned is the rise of a social class that helped to give Roman society a new stamp. "The old aristocracy of the city of Rome disappeared. New men came to replace them: some from municipal nobility of Italy, some from the more or less romanized provinces, some from the ranks of adventurers and favourites of the emperors."[1] In his essay of consolation to his mother, Seneca gives a vivid picture of the situation in the city. People have flocked here from everywhere—from the municipalities, from the colonies, from the four corners of the world. Some have been brought by ambition and some by public duty, while still others have been drawn by the opulence, the opportunity for study, and the spectacles. On the more idealistic side, friendship and the chance to express themselves have had an attraction for a number of outsiders.[2]

Drawn to Rome as if by a magnet, the foreigner wasted no time in pushing others aside to take advantage of the opportunity offered him. His influence was felt in every quarter, as Seneca or Juvenal can testify, and the immediate result was the rise of a new class of freedmen, who like Petronius' Trimalchio were rich and powerful but who substituted ostentation for breeding and culture. Much of the old Roman spirit, then, and many of the Republican traditions now gave way to an expanding Roman outlook. There were important ramifications for urbanity in all of this, for the purely

Roman stock and the noble Roman tradition with which Plautus, Lucilius, Cicero, and Horace had earlier connected *urbanitas* were now being diluted and replaced by this creeping cosmopolitanism.

Some change can be expected, then, but it is also important to realize that *urbanus* and *urbanitas* still continue in good use designating various aspects of sophistication, and that writers like Quintilian are still attempting to interpret such matters from a Ciceronian point of view. The rustic and foreigner are not forgotten either, for the man of Rome is quick to express himself on the shortcomings of each.

TO THE DEATH OF NERO

The tendency of *urbanus* and its cognates to take on broader connotations, which was evident in the Augustan period, is, if anything, intensified in this first century after Christ. It is clear from the way Petronius uses these terms in the *Satyricon*, for instance, that they can now connote a general refinement without implying anything exclusively Roman. Quartilla's maid, not without a note of irony in her voice, calls Encolpius and Ascyltus sophisticated young men (16), and a few paragraphs later (24) Quartilla herself uses the abstract as she speaks to Encolpius: "Oh you sharp fellow (*urbanitatis vernaculae*)! You really didn't realize that the *cinaedus* is an *embasicoeta*?" While she is certainly capitalizing on the Roman connotations of the abstract to create an ironic contrast with the Greek words, there is no reference here to Roman sophistication *per se*. In fact, if *vernaculae* is the correct reading, then it would tend to prove that *urbanitas* is losing its overtones of exclusiveness. When the abstract is qualified by an adjective elsewhere in the *Satyricon* (7) to denote what appears to be a stupid show of urbanity or a show of urbane stupidity (*urbanitate tam stulta*), the atmosphere is strikingly un-Ciceronian and seems to result from a colloquial use of the word to connote the naïveté and helplessness arising from the overly sophisticated life of the city.

These words show a similar tendency to take on more general connotations when they are applied to wit. While both can still imply a cleverness in matters of humor, thus recalling Domitius Marsus and his *urbana dicta*,[3] in some contexts there is a certain boldness or impudence implied. This, of course, is a perfectly natural extension of the idea of smartness and cleverness.[4] Valerius Maximus, for example, speaks of a "witty freedom" which he equates a little later to a "clever boldness" where in both cases the nouns that are used with the adjectives are quite startling.[5] As might be suspected, people can carry this kind of humor to an extreme which may at times be dangerous,[6] but which is always tasteless.[7] Sometimes this lack of control is so much a part of *urbanus* and *urbanitas* that it is difficult to see how the words can connote anything more than a general humor. Timagenes' derogatory comments involving Augustus, for instance, are called "reckless humor" by Seneca, while the philosopher also uses the abstract to describe insults that a slave mouths at the expense of his master.[8] *Urbanitas* is also used regularly to refer to the product of this humor, whether it be a clever joke or witticism[9] or whether it be simply a tasteless insult.[10]

From these examples it is quite clear that these words no longer designate anything that is peculiarly Roman. This was a perfectly natural semantic development, but it is also possible to see here another indication of the dissolution and disintegration of time-honored feelings and values as Roman sophistication and Roman wit were gradually buried under the avalanche of a growing cosmopolitanism.[11] It is more than a little ironic that these terms which earlier stood for refinement in a narrow Roman sense can now when properly qualified be made to apply to its diametric opposite. One instance of *urbanus*, however, which occurs in one of Phaedrus' fables (5.5.8) may retain at least a touch of Romanness, for when the city rake is described as being "well known for his urbane wit," Plautus' *urbanus scurra* with its peculiarly Roman overtones is immediately brought to mind.

Oddly enough, there is little or no direct reference to sophistication and urbanity in the literature of the period. This is not to say, however, that standards of urbanity were not recognized and fostered, for a mere mention of refinement calls to mind Petronius, the *arbiter elegantiae*, whose satiric novel is to a large extent a comment on the debasing of Roman sophistication. There is also the younger Seneca who in his treatises on Stoicism presents a refined approach to life based on philosophy.

But even though urbanity may not be discussed, the attitudes of the gentleman to those on the one hand who carry refinement to extremes and those on the other who fall short in such matters make their appearance frequently enough to show that at least some, if not all, of the earlier standards still exist. The city is criticized for the luxury and extravagance that is promoted there and so is the man who is too much a product of these tendencies. Seneca insists, for instance, that the better soldiers come from a rugged region, for "hands shifted from the plough to weapons of war refuse no work at all, while that elegant, perfumed [gentleman] breaks down at the first hint of work."[12] Elsewhere the philosopher includes "too dainty a sophistication" among those elements that feed anger[13] and makes still another pointed reference to the "overcultured crowd" when he contrasts it with the rough rabble.[14] Here he points out that the fops pamper themselves more than is right and necessary, even going so far as to shave their legs, while the riffraff do not even bother to shave their armpits. True urbanity presumably lies somewhere between these extremes.[15]

Earlier in this epistle Seneca has already provided an example of the kind of foppish extreme he means in the person of Maecenas: "How Maecenas lived is too well known to require a detailed account from me—how he walked, how effeminate (*delicatus*) he was, how he wanted everyone to look at him, how he never tried to hide his shortcomings." Slovenly dress, eunuch attendants, relations with his wife all come in for criticism and characterize a man who is soft and effeminate (*mollem*) rather than mild and gentlemanly (*mitem*).[16] It must be kept in mind that the whole purpose of this letter is to show how a person's verbal expression reflects his personality, so that there is the same connection between utterance and sophistication that Cicero had discussed earlier.

Attitudes to the countryman and his life are also part of a thoroughgoing urbanity at this time. In spite of the idealization of the rustic existence, which is often voiced by writers like Columella[17] and which comes mainly from a disenchantment with urban life, there is enough evidence to show that the urbanite viewed the countryman as realistically as he had earlier. As he discusses contemporary affluence, Seneca conveys the common opinion that "it is mere boorishness and misery to want only what is sufficient."[18] Behind this lies an attitude of the sophisticated Roman of the time who, because he cannot do without the products that wealth and affluence have brought, looks with contempt upon those who do not feel the same way. This boorishness is partly a naïveté, partly a lack of awareness, partly a stupidity.

An example of the kind of thing that the gentleman thought gauche is to be found in Scipio's habits of bathing which were not up to the standards of refinement that prevailed in the first century.[19] Though Seneca in this instance does not agree with what he considers to be an extreme attitude, it is clear from other random comments that for him the rustic represents a simplicity and ignorance that manifest themselves in an intense bashfulness,[20] a general lack of artistic skill,[21] an inexperience with books,[22] and an inability to understand subtle reasoning.[23] It comes as no surprise, then, to find that the adjective is now commonly used to designate ignorance and stupidity in general.[24]

To all of this should be added the fact that Seneca and other urbane Romans of the time found the rustic way of speaking no more acceptable than before. Evidence for this is the philosopher's description of proper use of the voice, in which he suggests that a change in tone from the vehement and violent to the gentle and restrained should be made gradually by having the voice glide and not by letting it fall in an uncouth, boorish manner (*indocto et rustico more*).[25] Evidently careful control of one's voice—perhaps it should be called a smoothness and flow—was usually missing in rustic utterance and so was open to criticism by the sophisticated Roman. But at the same time care must be taken not to read too much into the statement, since *rusticus* is used as a near synonym of *indoctus* and has surely lost many of its country connotations.[26]

Calpurnius Siculus has preserved what at first sight may appear to be a reliable picture of the countryman in a poem which begs comparison with Vergil's first *Eclogue*,[27] since both have as their subject the wide-eyed wonder that a rustic feels on his first visit to Rome. Here the similarity ends, however, for Vergil's rustic remains a rustic, while Calpurnius' speaker loses no time in expressing his dissatisfaction with the country and immediately begins an enumeration of the marvels of the city. As he goes through his list, it becomes apparent that the poet has not presented a real man from the farm, but an urban dweller in a rustic disguise whose purpose it is to mouth the poet's praise of urban things. The most that the poem has to offer, then, is evidence of a continuing recognition of the rustic as a simple type, thoroughly unacquainted with city ways.

Although he is not mentioned frequently, the uncultured foreigner was also the butt of the urbanite's criticism. After a long discussion of the wildness of barbarians, Seneca says: "If only that savagery had stayed within its foreign boundaries (*intra peregrina exempla*) and the barbarous punishments and other displays of anger had not made their way into Roman life along with other vices from outside."[28] He limits himself to examples from the past, but he surely has an eye on the uncouth manners and actions that he sees in the city.

Seneca's reservations are a little different from the prejudice expressed in a passage of the *Satyricon*. In answer to Encolpius' suggestion that Giton, Eumolpus, and he disguise themselves as

Ethiopian slaves, Giton immediately expresses his disapproval of this device by sarcastically proposing that they have themselves circumcised to look like Jews, have their ears pierced to look like Arabs, and have their faces chalked to look like Gauls. He goes on to ask whether they are able to achieve the other characteristics that would make them look like real Ethiopians—the thick lips, the curled hair, the scars, the gait, the beard trimmed in a foreign manner. Giton's feelings here very definitely foreshadow Juvenal's biting criticism of foreigners which was to appear almost half a century later.

At least one of the reasons for the urbanite's resisting the encroachment of the foreigner is to be seen in the recitation given by Habinnas' slave at Trimalchio's dinner (68). The terrible performance of this fellow, who is called a Jew by his master, is made even worse when he reveals his barbarous origin by raising and lowering his voice at the wrong time to produce the most unpleasant sound Encolpius has ever heard. It must have been a combination of servile birth, alien stock, poor education, and an innate stupidity that was responsible for this creature's terrible Latin.

Other comments are few and far between in this period. It is possible to conclude from an observation made by Calpurnius[29] that when the rustic is compared to the out-and-out barbarian he is a cut above him. Again, when Seneca in the *Apocolocyntosis* (3) makes humorous reference to Claudius' apparent desire to see all Greeks, Gauls, Spaniards, and Britons enfranchised, it is possible to find a contemporary rejection of the foreigner's encroachment on Roman privileges, though not necessarily on the Roman refinement. Finally, there is a comment of Seneca from exile[30] which has a particularly Ovidian ring about it. The writer apologizes in advance for any infelicities that might be found in this piece, for, he says, Latin words do not come easily to the person surrounded by a disjointed babble that is difficult for even the more civilized barbarians to bear. Though it would be dangerous to take his statement at face value, since it is an obvious attempt to evoke pity, the feeling of loathing for the barbarians expressed here is precisely that which appears in Ovid's poems from exile.

FROM VESPASIAN TO HADRIAN

A new era begins in Rome about the middle of the first century after Christ with a second civil war followed by reforms that were designed primarily to bring about a rebirth of the old Roman character. There is an emphasis on good administration, an extensive building program, and encouragement of literary activity that combine to make the last half of this century second only in achievement to Augustan times. But many years have passed during which the city and its people have undergone substantial change. Even a quick glance at the literature shows that, instead of another Cicero, there is Quintilian who believes he is following closely in the great orator's footsteps, but who in reality presents his public with a product peculiar to his own times. Juvenal may write in the satiric tradition of Lucilius and Horace, but he is the victim of the cosmopolitanism that he brands with his invective. Again, Pliny's letters are neither the spontaneous and informal efforts of a Cicero nor the philosophic literary creations of a Horace but a highly stylized product that falls somewhere between. In the case of Suetonius and Tacitus, both realize that the intervention of time and change has removed any possibility of their appreciating the epic sweep of Roman history as Livy had.

Feelings of urbanity and sophistication crop up often in the writers of this period. As a matter of fact, in these fifty years or so there is a greater variety of useful evidence than in any comparable length of time earlier. The city still presents an attractive image to inhabitant and outsider alike, as Tacitus shows when he observes that the poet who is to create anything substantial must leave the pleasant associations and attractions that Rome has to offer and find the peace, quiet, and solitude that promote such endeavors.[31] Because Rome is a fascinating place, people are still flocking there from Italy and the provinces, some of them simply to see and hear people whose reputation had reached them in their home towns,[32] but most of them to take up permanent residence in the city. Juvenal presents what must have been a fairly common reaction to this concentrated immigration when he screams out against Italians and foreigners alike who, though they come from lowly backgrounds, have gained wealth and reputation at Rome by using their wits and taking advantage of opportunities that have come their way.[33] When the intense coloring is removed from Juvenal's picture, it is possible to see an interesting interplay between the various elements in cosmopolitan Rome in which the true Roman's attitude is perfectly clear.

From time to time there is mention of incidents that stem from this rivalry. An interesting bit of repartee takes place between besiegers and besieged when the German soldiers of Vitellius are storming Placentia.[34] The city soldiery and praetorian cohorts, as they are called, taunt the Germans with being foreigners and aliens, and the attackers in turn gibe at the enemy's laziness and general sloth which they attribute to city living. A little later, when the army of Vitellius has encamped near Rome and the soldiers are receiving their rations, some of the people from the city, who have quite literally inundated the camp, go around cutting the soldiers' belts, thus disarming them without their knowing it.[35] When asked by these wags where their swords are, the soldiers fail to see the humor of the situation and slaughter the unarmed Romans. Though it is all but impossible to perceive anything sophisticated about these cityites and the joke they play, in spite of the fact that *urbanitas* is used to describe the prank, it is possible to see the friction between Roman and foreigner that must have been going on behind the scenes at Rome at this time.[36]

Feelings of sophistication manifest themselves in three different ways in the writers of the period. The poets Statius and Martial comment on urbanity out of a complete awareness of what it is and what its influence should be. Quintilian, on the other hand, returns to Cicero's point of view to attempt definition and description of *urbanitas* as it relates to rhetorical theory. Finally, there is Pliny the Younger who reveals himself as an ideal *urbanus homo* of the time in everything he does.

STATIUS AND MARTIAL

A glance through Statius' *Silvae* brings a feeling of being overwhelmed by the constant conscious effort on the part of the poet to produce an effect as full of delicacy, good taste, and cultivation as possible. Any attempt to select the one poem of the *Silvae* that best reveals itself as a product of urbanity immediately brings to mind Statius' hexameters on Vopiscus' villa at Tibur where the poet describes a magnificent home with fine furnishings set in an idyllic country atmosphere (1.3). Almost every line exudes refinement, and it is no wonder, for the piece is written by a sophisticated poet for a gentleman. Although it strikes a somewhat hollow note in the context, there is a reflection of the Ovidian cultivation without extravagance, when Statius characterizes all of this as "a sane-minded splendor and elegance without luxury" (92f.). In another poem, where essentially the same atmosphere prevails, there is a similar description of elegance and sophistication, this time as it emanates from Claudius Etruscus, the owner of the bath that Statius is so eloquently describing (1.5.63f.).

These two pieces not only stand as statements of urbanity, but also suggest that there is something forced and artificial about the contemporary Roman refinement, at least as it is interpreted by Statius. In spite of this, however, a closer look at the *Silvae* shows that *urbanitas* also manifests itself in much the same way as it had earlier. Statius' clever criticism of Grypus (4.9) begins with a rather blunt observation: "Yes, Grypus, that is your little joke (*iocus*) that you've sent me a little book in return for a little book. But this can seem clever, witty, and refined (*urbanum*) only if you send me something else as well . . . ." Here, right at the start, Statius neatly separates refinement in wit from humor in general by suggesting that there must be something clever and sophisticated about an attempt at humor if it is to stand on a higher plane. A careful reading of this poem brings the gradual realization that after drawing attention to urbanity of wit in the first few lines, the writer is actually giving an example of urbane wit at work, for not only is the whole poem an extremely clever tour-de-force, but at the end in what is almost a postscript there comes the cleverest cut of all: "Grypus, I am angry with you, but I wish you a farewell—[by the way,] just don't send me in return any hendecasyllabics [like these], in your usual witty way." There is no retort to this, for Statius has neatly made his point and has underlined it by showing Grypus what a real *urbanus iocus* is.

Besides recognizing urbanity as it manifests itself in a man's wit, Statius is fully conscious of other aspects of this refinement. During his fulsome praise of Septimius Severus in another of his *Silvae* (4.5.45f.), the poet makes the point that, in spite of his having been born at Leptis, he leaves an impression of being thoroughly Roman: "Your speech is not Carthaginian, nor are your clothes; your outlook is not that of a foreigner. You are an Italian! An Italian!" There can be no doubt that he is thinking of Rome when he uses the adjective *Italus*, for in the next breath he goes on to speak of the city. This is interesting, inasmuch as it shows that the Roman is at least beginning to equate Rome and Italy, even in matters of sophistication.

Martial's *Epigrams* are another expression of the Roman urbanity, inasmuch as they are in a direct line from Domitius Marsus and his epigrammatic *urbanitas*. The poet shows that he is fully conscious of this inheritance when he insists that he is writing for the urbane set in Rome and not for the stern and serious reader (11.16.1f.). He had made the same point a little differently in an earlier poem when he pictured the muse of epigram as advising him to "dip his little Roman books in pleasant, charming wit"

(8.3.19f.). Here the combination of Romanness and refined wit in essence connotes an *urbanitas*. It is no wonder, then, that Martial with typical epigrammatic understatement can call his book "hardly rustic at all" (*non rusticulum*) and judge it worth sending to a sophisticated gentleman like Pliny the Younger (10.20.1–4). Even when he is writing at Bilbilis after moving from Rome, he keeps his refined urban audience in mind, for he sends his book to Rome for the consul, the senate, and the knights (12.2.1–5), which together constitute a sophisticated circle of readers receptive to his poetry.

Although Martial is a poet of the city, who is well aware of the refinement and sophistication that is to be found there, he also recognizes its shortcomings and the compensations that country life has to offer. What bothers him most is the hecticity of urban life where all the professions, trades, and nationalities—teachers, bakers, coppersmiths, money-changers, soldiers, sailors, and even Jews—make up a wild conglomeration that prevents a man from finding peace and quiet.[37] It is no wonder, then, that he seconds Domitius on his way to the peace and quiet of Vercellae, where he will find relief from city burdens and take on a healthy color from country living, even though the unhealthy urban pallor can be expected to return to Domitius soon after he comes back.[38] It should be noticed that, like Horace, Martial does not advocate a rough and rustic life for the gentleman, but simply uses it as an escape from the undesirable conditions of the city.[39]

After he had spent some thirty-five years of his life in Rome, Martial did a surprising thing by returning to his native Bilbilis to live out his remaining years. This puts him in a unique position, for to this time there has been no one as apparently aware of and steeped in city sophistication who deserted it completely and moved so far away. Martial does not state his reasons for abandoning the city. It may have been that he was tired of the hustle and bustle that he so often criticizes, but it is also possible that after Domitian's death he found it the wise thing to do.

Whatever his motives, it is clear that he had never forgotten his native Spain all the time he was living in Rome, for his feelings of attachment to his native land keep appearing in his poems. As he contemplates Licinianus' trip to Spain (1.49), for instance, he savors the sights and scenes, and, though the picture is not quite ideal, there is a romantic emphasis on the peace, quiet, and simplicity of life in Bilbilis and the surrounding country.[40] Again, when he points to the contrast between Charmenion, the effeminate Corinthian, and himself (10.65), Martial's Spanish pride shows forth in quite a different way as he proudly tells this creature that he is an Iberian, a Celt, a citizen of the Tagus, and insists that he looks and sounds the part. In cosmopolitan Rome, then, a man no longer needs to apologize for his foreign birth, unless he is a Charmenion with his well-depilated appearance and effeminate utterance. Even before he returned to Spain, Martial hinted that he was thinking of doing so when, after an absence of thirty years, he addressed his people there (10.103), asking them if they appreciated his accomplishments. He ends this brief poem with the observation: "If you accept me back gratefully and peacefully, I'll come. But if you have negative feelings, I can always return to Rome."

While he went back to Bilbilis a few years later and ostensibly became a rustic again far from the hectic life of Rome (12.18), the initial feeling of euphoria does not seem to have lasted long, for in the letter prefaced to the twelfth book of the *Epigrams* Martial laments that he is in a foreign forum where he longs for the Roman audience which prompted his poetry. He misses their subtle judgment and their inspiration and he misses the accoutrements of this life—the libraries, theatres, and meeting places. A little later (12.21) he again expresses a longing for the city and describes how Marcella has done her best to create a Rome for him out here in Spain. There is a plaintive note once more in his address to his little book (12.2) as he speeds it on its way to the Subura and the house of the Consul Stella, who, Martial hopes, will read it with tear-filled eyes and pass it on to senate and knights. The refinement of the city has had a profound influence on the poet, and he cannot help but miss it. Although the intensity of feeling is not present, life in Bilbilis seems to have affected Martial in much the same way as Ovid's exile affected him.

Martial's pronouncements on people who are inurbane and boorish include criticism of Caecilius who may pride himself on being witty (*urbanus*), but who is actually no better than the lowest of the lowly as he spouts his jokes with unrestrained indelicacy.[41] Cotta who overdoes refinement may be brushed off in two lines as puny and insignificant (1.9), but Cotilus merits more attention. He is a well-perfumed, carefully coifed, hyperurbane dandy who not only lisps the latest tune from the Nile or from Gades, but dances lithely as well. He prefers to sit with the women, as he receives and sends his little notes, and will not let anyone touch him for fear his clothing will be soiled or disarranged. He knows the latest gossip which he presumably scatters as he hops from banquet to banquet. He is also "up" on his race horses.[42]

Martial does not comment often on the rusticity that lies at the opposite end of the scale, though he is fully aware of the *rusticus* and his inferiority. He chides Publius his host, for instance, for having too fine and cultivated a cupbearer and calls upon him to produce waiters that are short-haired, rough-and-ready sons of a smelly swineherd (10.98). He smiles at rustic ignorance as he describes the disastrous sacrifice made by the soothsayer and the countryman.[43] When in another context he warns the reader not to laugh at the names and places of Spain as being rustic, since there are boorish countrymen much closer to home, he is making oblique reference to the attitude of the sophisticated Romans to small towns in the backwoods of Spain and is at the same time revealing how he himself feels about people living in rural Italy (4.55.27 ff.).

From time to time Martial also expresses himself on the foreign element in Rome. People from all over the world have been attracted to the city in such numbers that they threaten to take over.[44]

124

A barbarian, for instance, feels no compunction about pushing a young citizen aside from the drinking fountain (11.96). But there is more to the influence than this, as Martial's criticism of Laelia shows, for she has cultivated a "Greekness," in spite of the fact that she is of Etruscan stock and has a hardy father who hails from Aricia (10.68). Martial's criticism of Laelia recalls Lucilius' picture of the Hellenophile Titus Albucius and shows that like his predecessors he cannot abide the undermining of the good old Roman morals and sophistication that is taking place.

Martial's gibes at the credulous Gaul (5.1.9f.) and at the dull and stupid Aquitanian (9.32.5f.) as well as his delightful sally against Charmenion the Corinthian (10.65) are all reflections of the same attitude to foreigners and the influence they are having in Rome. But with Martial there is a problem, since in the light of his feelings of partiality for Spain it is difficult to know how far his attitudes to foreigners stem from an awareness of Roman sophistication and to what extent they come from pride in his Spanish background. That both are at work is evident from the fact that he uses Roman culture as a point of reference for his criticism of Laelia but he becomes a Spaniard when he hits out at people like Charmenion.

QUINTILIAN AND *Urbanitas*

To move from Martial to Quintilian is to change the scene from the streets of Rome to the drawing room where rhetoric and its technical perfection hold sway. The *Epigrams* are occasional poetry which are meant as commentary and entertainment, while the *Institutio Oratoria* is a technical treatise in which description and definition are all-important. At first sight, Quintilian's attempts to analyze *urbanitas* and the conclusions he comes to seem to be remarkably Ciceronian, simply because much of what the orator had said is echoed here. But a closer look at the phenomenon as it appears in the *Institutio* brings increased awareness that in many ways it is quite different from the Republican concept. One of the clearest indications of this is the fact that *urbanitas* is nowhere used by Quintilian to denote a general refinement or culture, but is brought to bear in every instance on wit or speech.

Quintilian's most important observations on *urbanitas* are appended to his remarks on wit and humor in his sixth book (6.3.103–12). After quoting Domitius Marsus' definition of *urbanitas* and Cato's description of an *urbanus homo*, he criticizes them for their emphasis on brevity: "If we accept these definitions, whatever is said well will be labeled urbane." Quintilian does not like, or really understand, the application of the word *urbanitas* to smart, clever, epigrammatic *dicta*, since he views the abstract as something much less limited and much less easily defined.

This is immediately evident from his own definition (107) which reveals an *urbanitas* embracing just about every element of speech and oratory. It presupposes nothing incongruous, nothing country-fied, nothing confused, and nothing foreign in thought, vocabulary, pronunciation and intonation, and delivery, and Quintilian confirms all of this a few paragraphs later when he insists (110) that it is the over-all flavor of one's speech that reveals *urbanitas*. With this point of view Quintilian has moved from *urbanitas* as wit to *urbanitas* as refinement in speech, apparently basing what he says on Cicero's discussion in the *Brutus* (170 ff.). Not only does the terminology here sound suspiciously similar to that which Cicero uses, but the comparison with the flavor of Athenian speech that Quintilian makes calls quickly to mind the native flavor and the sound of Attic speech that are used for purposes of comparison in the *Brutus*.[45]

There is a striking similarity between this definition and an earlier one in which Quintilian has dealt with the kind of humor that he designates *urbanitas* (6.3.17), since in both cases there is the same emphasis on proper speech. In the earlier definition, however, Quintilian adds the observation that this combination of refined wit and utterance reveals the good taste that is characteristic of the city alone and leaves the unobtrusive impression of erudition.[46] It must also be noticed that in both contexts *urbanitas* finds its antithesis in rusticity.[47]

Quintilian has more to say about urbane wit at other points in his treatise. In his definitions he has already shown himself to be in a direct line from Cicero when he insists on restraint, moderation, and general propriety as the most important attributes of urbane wit. It is actually one of the most important epexegetic duties of the educator to elucidate written speeches for his young charges by pointing out and analyzing, among other things, this refinement in humor.[48] Following this dictum, Quintilian suggests that the skilled debater should avoid unbridled anger and bring a gracious wit into play instead (6.4.10), while elsewhere he asserts that, though humor put forward with a relatively serious facial expression may in many instances gain the desired results, yet a humorous look, expression, or gesture will be as successful, so long as the device is not carried to extremes.[49] What happens if moderation is not observed is evident from his warning that since hyperbole is a form of exaggeration, it will result not in tasteful humor (*urbanitas*) but in simple tomfoolery (*stultitia*), if it is carried beyond its potential.[50]

Propriety of application is also all-important, for a remark such as that which Augustus made about Marcianus in his presence would not have been classed as an *urbanum dictum* had it been made behind the subject's back (6.3.94f.). On another level this propriety may involve effectiveness. If *urbanitas* is applied at the right time and under the right circumstances, a difficult, self-possessed witness can be put off (5.7.26) or an opportune show of wit (*urbanitas opportuna*) can revive the jury and combat tedium that is bound to arise during a trial (4.1.49).

Quintilian's proposals as to how examples of urbane humor may be devised give a better idea of the nature of *urbanitas*. Though he conceives of wit as a general quality of a speech or utterance and opposes it to the smart remark labeled *urbanitas* by Marsus and

Cato, Quintilian does not rule out brevity as an effective means of producing it (6.3.45). As a matter of fact, most of his methods and examples do involve brief phrases, sentences, or short passages (6.3.96 ff.). A quoted verse that has been adapted to give a pun (96) or one in which a word has been replaced to produce an element of surprise (97) is of great help in generating successful humor, while proverbs, quotations from history and myth, and verses parodying well-known ones may also be put to good use (97 f.). At other points he suggests that a clever anecdote, such as the one Cicero tells about the elder Caepasius,[51] or pretended agreement with a sharp, unexpected rejoinder can be made to contribute materially.[52]

In each of the illustrations that Quintilian uses a feeling of irony is present to a greater or lesser degree so that it is not unreasonable to suppose that this is part of urbane wit.[53] It is certainly part of a show of wit by Caesar Vopiscus that Quintilian describes in some detail (6.3.38). When one Helvius Mancia insisted on interrupting him as he spoke, Caesar warned him that if he did not stop he would show him what he was. When Mancia, in turn, insisted that he show him, Caesar turned without a word and pointed to the head of a Gaul painted on a Cimbrian shield which hung as a sign over a shop nearby. This is urbane wit at its best, for not only is it a subtle, clever insult, but the insult consists in Caesar's striking at Mancia's feelings of urbanity and Romanness by silently suggesting that he is a noisy, nasty Gaul. It is impossible not to admire this show of sophisticated wit at the expense of another man's sophistication.

Before leaving this aspect of urbanity it should be pointed out that Quintilian also employs the abstract *urbanitas* to designate the product of this refined wit, the joke or witticism, as his immediate predecessors had. In what is perhaps the most informative occurrence, the fact that *urbanitas* is almost synonymous with *iocus opportunus* shows that it stands for a witticism that is particularly appropriate in regard to both time and place and very likely context.[54]

That Quintilian finds a close alliance between urbanity of wit and urbanity of speech is clearly evident from his general definition of urbane wit where he puts special emphasis on thought, vocabulary, pronunciation and intonation, and even gesture (6.3.107). Elaboration of each of these elements appears from time to time in Quintilian's treatise. His insistence that there be nothing rustic in the manner of a man's delivery recalls his mention much earlier that awkward, rustic use of the hands should be avoided (1.11.16). The lad from the country in stereotype always suffers from not knowing what to do with his hands, and Quintilian is probably thinking of some such awkwardness as this. Elsewhere he says that he has seen a supposedly able orator employing movements that one would not expect even from a rustic (11.3.117)— demanding a cup, brandishing a lash, or raising one's fingers to represent the number 500. In his observation that foreign schools teach gestures that are overly dramatic and must be avoided at all costs (11.3.103), there is another reflection of the feeling that lies behind his definition.

Again, assiduous attention must be given to vocabulary, word arrangement, and usage at all times (8.1.1 ff.). Taken individually, words must not only be Latin and carefully chosen, but they must be used with proper emphasis and suited to their purpose, while in composition they should be correctly related to one another, carefully arranged, and harmoniously phrased. Quintilian would demand vocabulary that has as little foreign about it as possible, but it is interesting to notice that the Latin of the whole of Italy and not just that of the city is now considered Roman for his purposes (1.5.55 f.). With all of this Quintilian jolts the reader away not only from the Ciceronian concept of *urbanitas*, but from Cicero's more general views on language, for the orator could never have agreed to such a broad statement as that which is presented here. Words that are foreign in Quintilian's eyes are mainly Greek, though he also rejects Gallic, Carthaginian, and Spanish vocabulary.[55]

When he comes to pronunciation and tone of voice, Quintilian does not seem to attempt to separate the two as Cicero had done. Late in the *Institutio* (11.3.30) he mentions a way of speaking that is flowing (*os facile*), distinct (*explanatum*), pleasant (*iucundum*), and refined (*urbanum*), in which there is no sound of rusticity or foreignness. When he goes on to compare the sound of men's speech to the ring of a coin (31), not only does it become clear that the writer is thinking throughout this passage of a combination of vocal timbre and pronunciation, but the vocabulary recalls that used by Cicero in the *Brutus* when he is describing these aspects of a man's utterance.[56] And so it seems likely that Quintilian means to describe a nearly ideal manner of speaking which flows because of careful pronunciation and a pleasant tone of voice, thus leaving an overall impression of refinement.

He apparently has these matters in mind when in his lament over the death of his son[57] he points to the boy's having "a pleasant clarity of voice" and "a sweetness of utterance," and goes on to mention the child's careful way of pronouncing Latin. Because the latter is very important, Quintilian insists that the teacher give particular attention to it by combating that which is thin or over-rich and heavy, and by seeing to it that the harsher sounds (*acriores*) get their full pronunciation.[58] Moreover, the teacher is not to allow his student's simple and natural way of speaking to be overspread by "a broader kind of sound" which is fatal to pure speech. Quintilian may be thinking of the same thing as Cicero was when the orator criticized Cotta for his flat rustic pronunciation, and, although Quintilian's explanation of this fault in the following lines is not clear, the *plenior sonus* which is to be avoided would appear to be the same low-pitched, dull-sounding, and flat way of speaking.

These, then, are Quintilian's observations on urbanity that can be gleaned from the *Institutio,* and there now remains the obvious task of comparing what he says on the subject with what Cicero had said earlier. While the point has been made often enough that he apparently has Cicero's pronouncements in mind as he writes, Quintilian's estimate of *urbanitas* seems in retrospect to be quite different from that of his predecessor. In matters of humor, he reveals the later tendency to make *urbanitas* more tangible and much more easily defined, so that it is now possible for him not only to include in his treatise a lengthy analysis of this phenomenon with some definition but also to outline the methods by which it may be acquired. Nothing so elaborate was attempted by Cicero, since this humor for him was part of a larger refinement which was to be felt rather than described. *Urbanitas* is now no longer the exclusive city wit so elusive of definition, then, but a more general refined humor which can be a topic in a textbook for the person who wishes to acquire the credentials of a well-educated man.

In his definitions Quintilian clearly equates *urbanitas* and refined speech in all its aspects, at the same time insisting that through this the gentleman not only reveals that certain good taste which is characteristic of the city alone but also leaves the unobtrusive impression of learning acquired from direct contact with those who are *docti*. Herein lies another fundamental difference between Cicero's conception of *urbanitas* and that of Quintilian, for the later writer is describing formal speech or oratory which belongs to one group of Romans, the educated, and which for him is the end purpose, even the climax, of the educative process. Because of the equation which Quintilian makes, urbanity becomes the whole aim of education as it is outlined in the *Institutio Oratoria*.[59] This *urbanitas* is far different from its Ciceronian counterpart, which was a nebulous something which could be heard but not described, and which was for the most part a natural inheritance and not something to be achieved by any amount of formal education. To reduce the contrast to simpler terms: The *totius orationis color* of Quintilian is the perfect *sermo* of the perfect orator, while Cicero's *urbanitatis color* is an intangible and almost magical attribute of city speech, formal and informal alike, that sets it off from the utterance of any extraurbanite, no matter how well educated he may be.

There is one point, however, on which Cicero and Quintilian are in complete agreement. Urbane wit and urbane speech, though they may be discussed separately, are not separate entities or concepts. This was perfectly clear when the Ciceronian urbanity was discussed earlier, and Quintilian's definitions show that it is still the case. The narrow, national urbanity, obscure and ill defined, may have yielded to a broad, impersonal, cosmopolitan refinement, but *urbanitas* is still considered to be a single unit.

PLINY THE YOUNGER

There can be little doubt that if Quintilian were asked to choose the Roman who came closest to his ideal of *urbanitas*, he would select Cicero. Pliny, however, would be a close second. Martial respected this man for his refinement (10.20.1–5), and Trajan's replies to his communiqués from the east are those of one *urbanus homo* to another. But Pliny's urbanity presents problems for anyone attempting to analyze it within the limits imposed by the present study, since there is a superabundance of evidence in the letters. At the same time, there is no clear statement of what constitutes this refinement, apparently because Pliny and his contemporaries took it so much for granted. In spite of these difficulties, however, by carefully selecting the evidence, it is possible to get some idea of Pliny's urbanity and that of the people with whom he associated.

The fact that *urbanitas* appears only twice in Pliny's letters is surely an indication that the term had all but outlived its usefulness as an indicator of something exclusive and unique. In one instance the word is used to signify the element of humor that is an important part of rhetorical training, while in the other it suggests a clever, presumably ironic wit that Pliny felt had no place in the deliberations of the senate.[60] In neither case does it describe anything that is uniquely Roman. And this is not surprising, for the spontaneity which characterized life in the Republic and gave birth to terms like *urbanitas* has given way to a view of life governed by a deliberate sense of propriety which at times places its values in the mediocre. In this atmosphere, therefore, *urbanitas* no longer connotes a feeling that must be fostered and defended at all costs. This is not to say that refinement has disappeared, however. It is just that Pliny, a gentleman *par excellence* of his time, shows clearly what has become increasingly evident—the old, narrow concept of a purely Roman exclusiveness and urbanity no longer exists.

Most of the examples of *urbanus* will be best considered as they come naturally into the discussion later, but two instances serve to underline what has already been said. One occurrence (5.6.35) of the superlative shows that Pliny is conscious of the refinement that still clings to the word, for he uses it to describe a formal planting at his Tuscan villa and contrasts this with the kind which he would label rustic. The application of the word in this context recalls the elder Pliny's use of the term to describe cultivated trees and represents a late usage that is hardly Ciceronian in flavor.[61]

In the second instance (4.25.3) it occurs along with the adjective *dicax* and *bellus* describing a person who has misused the new system of balloting in the senate. The same connotations of irony and sarcasm are present as they were earlier, but here *urbanus* has become just another word for somebody or something that is humorous. In fact, the humor that is involved is not in Pliny's eyes dreadfully respectable, as his use of *scurriliter* shows.

Many cultured men are described or discussed in the letters, for Pliny prided himself on having a great number of friends, most of whom were gentlemen. In a letter to Fabatus, his wife's grandfather (6.30.3–5), who has evidently asked him to recommend an overseer for an estate, Pliny points to the fact that Fabatus is looking for someone who is rough and rustic to do the job, and his friends do not have these qualifications. "I do seem to have a great number of acquaintances," he says, "but hardly anyone of the kind which you want and the situation demands. All of my friends are city gentlemen" (*togati et urbani*). This is the circle in which Pliny moves, and it is with a touch of pride that he offers his excuse to Fabatus.

Perhaps the best discussion of one of these gentlemen is to be found in a letter to Arrius Antoninus (4.3), where, after pointing to this man's political honors and position in the state and after underlining his deep sense of honesty in his public life, Pliny goes on to his personal, nonadministrative virtues. Arrius reveals a sternness (*severitas*) tempered with an affability (*iucunditas*) and a dignity (*gravitas*) coupled with a sense of courtesy (*comitas*),[62] combinations, Pliny asserts, which are difficult for any but a few to achieve. Added to these is an "unbelievable charm (*suavitas*) which is revealed in his conversation and in his writing." This observation naturally leads to rather profuse praise of Arrius' Greek epigrams and mimes. The eulogy of *comitas* here may recall the combination *comis et urbanus* which was used by Horace. But even without such an association, the overtones of urbanity cannot be missed. Arrius exhibits a combination of characteristics that have been associated with the *urbanus homo* in earlier times—successful administration, a temperament showing a proper balance between sternness and aloofness on the one hand and affability and courtesy on the other. Everything he says, everything he writes, and everything he does reveals this urbanity.

Other men who appear in the letters show similar combinations of good qualities. Quintianus maintains a balance between *gravitas* and *comitas* that is surely a decorum of habit and behavior with which urbanity can be equated (9.9.2). In Priscus (7.15.3) there is a simple honesty (*simplicitas*) and sense of courtesy (*comitas*), while Spurinna (3.1.9) is a refined old man whose meals are characterized by an affability and politeness (*comitas*). Again, Fannia (7.19.7) is a charming (*iucunda*) and polite (*comis*) person. Nowhere in these comments does Pliny say that this is a

Roman refinement, but perhaps it is not necessary that he do so, since he is a Roman writing about Romans. Moreover, it is possible to assume Roman overtones from his use of *gravitas, severitas,* and the like, since these are time-honored Roman virtues. Great care must be taken in making this kind of supposition, however, since *severitas, comitas,* and even *gravitas* are enumerated as character-istics of people like the philosopher Euphrates who come from as far away as Syria (1.10. esp. 1–8). In the case of the latter, it is tempting to conclude not only that *urbanitas* has given way to the all-enveloping cosmopolitanism, but that the *urbanus homo* is being replaced by the *homo humanus.*

The details of this refinement appear mainly as before in the way a man speaks and in the wit he uses. In the case of Arrius Anton-inus, as has already been noticed, Pliny made special mention of a sweetness in his utterance. Another urbane man, the youthful Fuscus Salinator, is described as having the combination of *gravitas* and *comitas* that was noted in the other *urbani.* In his case, how-ever, there is much more emphasis on his interest in the externals of the urbane life which include country living, study, and correct speaking (6.26.1). Pliny devotes a whole letter (9.36), presumably in answer to Fuscus' queries, to describing how he spends a day at his Tuscan villa, and it is obvious from a later letter (9.40) that Fuscus was interested enough in this aspect of a gentleman's life to ask further how the regimen at the Tuscan and Laurentine villas differ. Elsewhere (7.9) Pliny makes his recommendations for study, once again in reply to a petition from the younger man, and it is during this discussion that one of the two instances of *urbanitas* (13) appears. Fuscus gives every indication, then, of wanting to become familiar with what constitutes the life of refinement. He evidently has already learned some of his lessons well, for Pliny describes him as an eloquent young man (6.26.1) who uses ap-propriate gestures (*decorus habitus*), has a strong voice, and speaks with a pure Latin (6.11.2). While it is dangerous to read too much into these comments, it is possible to see in Fuscus an *urbanus homo*–orator such as Quintilian was trying to create. Pliny's praise of Fuscus here and his comment on Arrius' speech mentioned earlier recall the characterization of Voconius Romanus, whom Pliny finds very attractive because of "a marvelous sweetness in his speech and in his appearance."[63]

The gentleman in the letters who is perhaps best known for his sophisticated humor is Atilius Crescens. Writing to Priscus, Pliny describes him as an ideal conversationalist who whenever he opens his mouth combines a charm or sweetness of utterance with a pleasant wit (6.8.7). Evidently this refined sense of humor is extremely important, for the writer asks Priscus to get Crescens' money for him so that his naturally happy outlook will not become one of gloom, "for, after all, you know the witty ways (*facetias*) of this man" (6.8.8). An example of Crescens' wit has survived in his observation that "it is better to be doing nothing than to be accomplishing nothing" which struck Pliny as being very witty (1.9.8). In this clever, smart remark, the point of which resides in the contrast between *otiosum* and *nihil agere,* it is obvious that standards of urbane humor have not changed to any great extent. This kind of wit had its place in more formal contexts as well, as Pliny's comments on the comedy of Vergilius Romanus and on the lyric poetry of Passennus Paulus show.[64] In the realm of oratory, Homullus on at least one occasion spoke cleverly, pointedly, and urbanely.[65]

These are not by any means all the references to urbane men and urbanity that appear in the letters, but they are enough to show that the *urbanus homo* is very much in evidence in this period and that his standards of urbanity, as in earlier times, are reflected in the way he behaves and speaks and in the impression that his wit leaves with others. Even a cursory reading of the letters brings the realization that Pliny exhibits the same good qualities that he attributes to these men. His show of anger in a letter to Paulinus (2.2), for instance, is not simply an uncontrolled outburst, for, even though he begins with a strong, flat statement, he qualifies it almost at once, softens it further as the letter proceeds, and ends on the pleasant, positive note of an urbane and cultured man: "I am enjoying my studies and I am relishing just being lazy at my villa." There is no tirade, though the writer seems to threaten one at the beginning, and yet he leaves no doubt that he is angry. In this letter, then, Pliny shows the combination of sternness and affability or politeness which he admired in men of urbanity like Arrius Antoninus and Fuscus Salinator.

Pliny's confession that he enjoys lower forms of humor and that he indulges in humorous trivia himself from time to time (5.3.2) must be put in the proper perspective. Genitor has evidently complained of being present at a banquet that in all respects was very fine, except that the comic entertainment afterwards was less than sophisticated. In a letter to him (9.17) Pliny agrees that such low entertainment as the soft, salacious humor of a pervert, the unsubtle cleverness of a buffoon, and the stupidity offered by a fool are not really acceptable to him either. He prefers more subtle and refined entertainment—a clever reader, a lyric poet, or a comedian. Pliny the sophisticate, then, expects his entertainment and the humor contained in it to be commensurate with his own refinement and learning, but at the same time he admits a certain broadmindedness in his application of this philosophy. He does not find the low material entirely unacceptable, and does not suggest that it be done away with, but recognizes the fact that this kind of thing does have an appeal for some people. It should, therefore, be tolerated in the hope that those with different tastes will in turn be tolerant of what Genitor and Pliny like.

Pliny's views on the relationship between city and country also provide insights into his idea of the makeup of Roman urbanity. He often speaks out against the kind of life that must be endured in the city, using complaints which for the most part are the traditional ones. At the same time he balances these feelings with an affection and a longing for the rustic scene as a place of peace, quiet, and retreat. The city life is fraught with nuisances (*moles-*

tias), while the country is a place of leisure (*otium*) and pleasures (*voluptates*), where a man may arise when he chooses, wear what he likes, and spend the day doing what pleases him. Pliny puts these thoughts forward as part of a quietly humorous rebuke of Praesens for being absent from Rome for so long (7.3). At the same time he offers him congratulations on being able to stay away, for the only reason that he can offer him for coming back is to season "that very pleasant way of life [in the country] with more pungent herbs, so to speak, from time to time." The peaceful retirement of country life, then, must not be allowed to become routine and so be taken for granted.

This same contrast is put in slightly different terms in a letter to Fundanus (1.9) where the writer describes city life as a continual round of attendance at private ceremonies, official functions, or at the law courts. When a person is engaged in this kind of thing, he thinks it is important, but when he looks at it from the proper perspective, it all seems useless and senseless. Pliny finds this proper perspective when he has retired to his Laurentine estate, for there he is not subject to malicious gossip, rumor, and emotional problems caused by constantly being on the razor's edge of hope and fear. This life is the "true and pure life," and it is "leisure sweet and honorable." But health of body and soul is not the only reason for seeking out this leisure, since the mind also benefits from the simple fact that here in the country it is possible to find the time for reading, meditation, and composition that does not exist in town.

By this time, the dichotomic life had become routine for most urbane Romans, and it was so taken for granted that the gentleman would spend a fair amount of time in his country retreat that the word *secessus* had come to signify the place to which he withdrew. And so, when Pliny the Elder is described as dividing himself between his pursuits "amid the trials, tribulations and noise of the city" and those *in secessu* (3.5.14), it is certainly the city-country balance that is meant. At this time the gentleman must have been spending more and more time away from Rome. Terentius Junior, a man of equestrian rank, is an example of a person who has achieved a certain success in the city but has become disgusted with urban life and has retired to his country retreat (7.25.3–6). Upon receiving an invitation to his villa, Pliny has certain misgivings, since he does not know what to expect, and so, assuming Terentius to be a venerable farmer, he prepares himself for a discussion of rustic matters. Pliny is pleasantly surprised, however, to find that his host is an educated man with a broad intellectual background who speaks excellent Latin and Greek. His comment at this point is significant: "You would think he was a man living in Athens, not at a villa."

There are overtones of Horatian feelings in Pliny's address to Gallus at the end of his long description of his villa at Laurentum (2.17.29), for this fellow, like Horace's Aristius Fuscus, is one of those confirmed urbanites who have difficulty seeing anything attractive about life in the country. Apparently he has expressed some wonder that Pliny takes such delight in this estate, so that at the end of the letter, Pliny takes him to task for being too wrapped up in the city life: "If you don't have any desire for a country retreat, you are just too urbanized" (*tu nimis urbanus es*). Pliny's comment is important, since it shows that a man with the right kind of sophistication is expected to maintain a proper blend of country living and city living. It should be noticed as well that there is a certain group of Romans who still believe that living in the sophisticated atmosphere of the city takes precedence over anything else.

But Pliny shows that he is fully aware of the fact that the rustic life is not all ease and study when he balances these pleasures against the hard work that is to be found there (9.10.3). Out of these contrasting themes come two different stances or attitudes of Pliny, depending on the person to whom he is writing.[66] It is Pliny the laboring, conscientious businessman-farmer who writes Calvisius Rufus (3.19) for financial advice in connection with the possible purchase of a tract of land adjoining his estate. Here he carefully lays the pros and cons of this business venture before his friend. In another letter to Calvisius (8.2), Pliny describes his struggle to sell the year's vintage and his attempts to cope with financial difficulties arising from it. When he mentions his attempts to solve this problem and those arising between him and his tenants in the matter of leases (9.37), it is evident that Pliny is imaginatively experimenting with new approaches and obviously putting much time and thought into such matters.

But the difficulties with the tenants here recall passages in other letters where a more irritable Pliny makes his presence felt. Typical of this less patient approach are the author's complaints to Genitor (7.30) where, after grumbling that his urban business has followed him into the country, he laments the fact that the rustics are becoming restless because he has been a long time getting to their complaints. Another distasteful task that awaits him is that of finding suitable tenants to whom he can lease his lands. When the reason for his impatience comes out—these problems and tasks distract him from his studies—it is obvious that Pliny is an educated, urbane nonrustic talking to a similarly cultured gentleman about rustic problems. For both of them the country is primarily a place of pleasure and leisure for study that is not to be interrupted by realities.

Pliny's mood here calls to mind another passage in which the author expresses a distaste for such matters in much the same way (5.14.8). He is making a tour of what he calls his "little holdings" (*agellos*) in company with his wife's grandfather and aunt, and as they walk around, he listens to the complaints of his rustics and thumbs account books. All of this he does unwillingly, for he wants to leave the impression that he is a sophisticated gentleman who really has no interest in country problems and the details of running a farm.[67] But there is a beneficial side to all this, for the fact that he has to spend his valuable time on these rustic complaints makes him all the more appreciative when he finds the time to pursue his literary studies and other cultivated interests (9.36.6). This letter takes on a special importance from the fact that here

Pliny puts forward his idea of life in the country as a harmony of composition, meditation, exercise, and sophisticated entertainment, all developed in an aura of peace, quiet, and leisure.

The impression that these comments of Pliny leave is confirmed in other letters. Writing to Baebius (1.24), he gives Suetonius' specifications regarding the purchase of a little farm (*agellum*) which must be close to Rome and should have good access roads, a rather small house, and a moderate amount of land. In this way, Suetonius will be diverted but not harassed by it, for he is, after all, a scholar, and his primary need is for a place to refresh soul, body, and mind. This, of course, is not Pliny's idea of a *secessus*, but it is surely typical of what many sophisticated men of the time envisioned the country as being.

In line with this is a picture of the vintage on one of his estates which neatly contrasts with what he says to Calvisius about another vintage (8.2). "I am harvesting the vintage . . . if indeed you can call it harvesting," for, as he goes on to say, he is just picking the odd grape, looking in on the press, and wandering around to speak to his city slaves who really have no time for him since they are busy helping the rustics. Here is Pliny the landowner making token visits to the *labores ruris* but remaining aloof from it all.[68]

Pliny, then, has two contrasting *personae* when he views the country. In one he is the hard-working, interested landholder, while in the other he plays the educated, urbane country squire with no use for the activities and problems of rustic life. Any attempt to decide which is the right picture presents serious difficulties, though most people would probably believe that the real Pliny exists in the first *persona*, and the Pliny that his sophisticated fellows would like to see in the second *persona*. Wherever the truth may lie, the clearest picture of Pliny as an urbane gentleman comes from his comments on city-country relationships and on the problems and pleasures of rural living.

It is perhaps worth insisting once again that no attempt has been made to carry out a thorough study of Pliny's refinement. The letters themselves deserve more attention as products of Pliny's urbanity, for a gentleman's expression, whether oral or written, could be expected to reveal his refinement. Because there is no time to go into a detailed discussion of the letters from this point of view, it is hoped that it will be sufficient to observe that each in language, subject matter, and general atmosphere faithfully reflects the sophistication of its writer. In this respect they are remarkably like the Dialogues of Plato which were discussed earlier.

Before leaving Pliny, it is necessary to compare his later concept of urbanity with Cicero's Republican outlook. Justification for this lies partly in the fact that Pliny thought he was emulating his eminent predecessor in matters of rhetoric and oratory (1.5.12) and in at least one instance suggests a comparison and contrast that is to be made between their letters (9.2.2). It is tempting to go a step further and imagine that Pliny saw a similarity on the personal level, for as an orator, lawyer, administrator, poet, and letter writer with erudite, sophisticated interests he had much in common with Cicero.

But whether Pliny felt this way or not, the two can be compared simply because each presents himself as an *urbanus homo* of his time. It is not surprising that the impression of urbanity left by Cicero is far different from that left by Pliny, for they represent contrasting personalities living in different eras. Both wrote letters that reflected their urbanity, but the two creations are hardly alike. Cicero wrote in a period fraught with peril when there was much to write about and when the letter was still a spontaneous form of expression, characterized by a tasteful informality that set it apart as a literary creation in its own right. Pliny's letters, on the other hand, because they are synthetic and contrived, lack this spontaneity and have become in effect brief essays on a variety of subjects written as literary exercises first and human communication second.

In a way, each set of letters reflects the urbanity from which it springs. The point has been made often enough that for Cicero *urbanitas* is something natural and innate in the Roman gentleman's character which cannot really be defined. But Cicero does not worry too much about his inability to describe it, since he knows it is there because he senses it. Pliny could never feel this way about his urbanity. For him it is something that he must constantly and consciously present to an audience. In nearly every one of his letters he sets out some aspect of this sophistication, whether it comes as a direct observation or as an implication from the subject matter, and by doing so this gentleman reveals that, as with everything else in his life, urbanity is a matter of conscientious study. It becomes what has been called an intense "tendency to conform."[69] This is a proclivity of an age which is reacting to the license and excess of the Julio-Claudian period which preceded.

But another influence that makes itself felt at this time in Pliny's views on urbanity and sets him apart from Cicero is the movement, feeling, or tendency that is designated *humanitas*. It is most clearly in evidence in his attitude toward the Christians, and it must have been reinforced by the ever-increasing cosmopolitanism of the first century which made the Roman more aware than ever before that he was part of a world that extended far beyond the walls of Rome and the shores of Italy. In Cicero's time, there was a *humanitas* and it played an important part in Roman thinking. The Roman had become increasingly aware of it since the first contact with Greek literature some two centuries earlier. But the area of experience and application was still circumscribed, and the man of Rome was only beginning to notice people living outside the city and its immediate sphere of influence. Cicero was still a *Romanus* in the sense that he advocated an isolation from any influence from without, and as such he was a true *urbanus homo*. Pliny, on the other hand, is an *urbanus homo* when the city is taken as the point of reference, but he is also a member of a much wider world in which he becomes a *homo humanus*.

EPILOGUE

Some attempt must be made to trace *urbanitas* in later Roman times to avoid the implication that it suddenly disappeared in the early years of the second century. A detailed treatment is out of the question, however, for the simple reason that it would demand another volume comparable in size to this one. Even a cursory glance through the Roman writers of the second century after Christ leaves the impression that urbanity was very much in their minds and that many of the earlier ideas about it carried on. *Urbanus* is used by Gellius, for instance, with connotations of a clever, refined wit firmly based on learning when he joins it to *facetus* to describe a witty remark of Cicero[1] and when he refers to a particularly humorous remark of a contemporary praetor.[2]

Urbanitas also appears from time to time. In Apuleius' *Metamorphoses* it is the sum total of all those characteristics that enable the gentleman to leave the proper impression on those with whom he associates, though it is more than a little surprising to find that it is a Greek Byrrhaena who is here attributing these qualities to Thelyphron, another Greek. In spite of this, there can be no doubt that the abstract has many of the same connotations it had earlier, since Apuleius goes on to connect it through *comitas* with "the charm of sophisticated speech."[3] It may be that the writer is smiling in the direction of his fellow Roman sophisticates as he pens these words.[4]

The *urbanus homo* appears in the *Metamorphoses* in the person of the hero Lucius who is certainly a figment of Apuleius' imagination, but whose refinement is genuine. This is especially evident in the first few books where Lucius is portrayed in terms that remind us of the typical young hero of Greek Romance. He is called a man of rank (*vir ornatus*) because of his clothes and his behavior (1.20), and he exhibits good manners that take many forms. Out of respect for the opposite sex, for instance, he finds it impossible to take a chair from a lady, even though he has been urged to do so, so that Milo is prompted to call him a born gentleman (23: *generosa stirpe*). A few paragraphs later Lucius shows his refinement and general *savior faire* once again when he succeeds in excusing himself with grace and courtesy (*comiter*) from a meal which he has no desire to attend (1.26). Apuleius' gentleman deserves more detailed treatment, and careful comparison with the heroes of Greek Romance would almost certainly yield interesting and profitable results, but the instances cited will serve to show for the present how the writer conceived of him.

The *urbanus homo* of the second century after Christ is seen even more clearly in the personalities of Fronto and Aulus Gellius. Fronto's *urbanitas* reveals itself on almost every page of his letters, for he works as hard at playing the gentleman as Pliny had earlier. He is a well-educated man who fully appreciates the finer things of life, and, because he is a teacher, he feels an obligation to instill an appreciation of such things in those to whom he is writing. As a gentleman he not only values the city, but is also well aware of the joys of retreating to Baiae or to a country estate. His correspondents are likewise sophisticated men who have these same interests,[5] and because some of them are among the most important men in the state—Antoninus Pius and Marcus Aurelius stand out—the respect they show for Fronto and his sophistication takes on a certain significance. Specific examples of Fronto's urbanity are easily found. His cleverness is perhaps best seen in his eulogy of dust and smoke and in his praise of negligence, which represent a new vehicle for urbane wit.[6] It would appear that declamation with its emphasis on the new and the different has had its effect, and when Fronto indulges in this kind of activity he stamps himself as belonging to the second century.

Other aspects of Fronto's urbane outlook will be mentioned in the paragraphs which follow, but it should be pointed out here that, even though he seems to imagine himself as being in a direct line from Cicero and Pliny, the results show that this is not the case. He has next to nothing in common with Cicero, and, while at times his letters are reminiscent of those of Pliny, Fronto has moved away from his predecessor in outlook, just as Pliny represents a stage of development that is a step beyond Cicero. It may be matters of personality that cause the difference, but there also seems to be less consciousness and appreciation of the details of sophistication. The veneer is there, but the spontaneity and exclusiveness are slipping away.

Aulus Gellius reveals himself as a gentleman as he puts together his medley of bright stories, observations, and anecdotes which are meant to appeal primarily to the refined set of Rome. In the preface to the *Noctes Atticae* (10) the writer, after disclaiming any interest in "charming" titles, insists that he has chosen his rather carelessly and has applied no great amount of thought to the matter. There may therefore be something "rather boorish" (*subrustice*) about it. But the reader knows and Aulus Gellius knows that writers do not work in this way. As a matter of fact, when this title is compared with those attached to works of similar content (and Gellius has provided a long list to make the comparison easy [*Praef.* 6–9]), it is immediately apparent that his choice is cleverly different not only because it is simpler than most but also because it only indirectly describes the content. It is dangerous to imagine that Gellius the gracious, self-effacing gentleman really means to have his appraisal of his title taken at face value.

Two other comments later in the *Noctes Atticae* suggest why he would not seriously qualify anything of his as being boorish. It is Aulus Gellius the *urbanus homo* once again who asserts that a person who prefers a speech of Gracchus to the *Second Verrine* must have a rustic, unsophisticated ear.[7] He may be thinking of the same failing when he uses these words a few books later to describe the man who has no appreciation of the more subtle sounds of Latin.[8] The writer's attitude to what is obviously a lack of sophistication cannot be missed in these comments.

The purposes of his work as he outlines them in the preface also smack of *urbanitas*, for Gellius is attempting to reach the man who has the education and the leisure to appreciate and benefit from the kind of material he is putting together. He insists that he is not trying to write for the person who, because he is completely wrapped up in his business, has no time for such matters (19). He realizes, moreover, that it is fruitless to try to communicate through such a medium with those who are poorly educated (20: *male docti*). His audience has to be of an extremely high caliber simply because his primary purposes are to spur a man's genius, help his memory, improve his eloquence and diction, give him pleasure in his idle hours, and bring a refinement to his amusements (16). In other words, Gellius means to add to his readers' learning and sophistication. Throughout his work he plays the dilettante, collecting and editing material that he believes will have the influences that he has outlined in his preface.

His most important pronouncements on urbanity involve speech, for the *urbanus homo* still seems to be especially interested in the quality of the voice and the fine art of conversation. It has already been noted that Thelyphron's *urbanitas* in the *Metamorphoses* is evidenced by his "charming conversation" (*lepidus sermo*), and that Byrrhaena is extremely eager to hear him talk. Gellius suggests a formula for such conversation when he puts forward with tacit acceptance Varro's prescription for a banquet (13.11.4f.) which was discussed in an earlier chapter. In this Menippean satire which Gellius describes as "very charming" (*lepidissimus*), Varro suggests that guests talk neither too much nor too little and that their conversation be not serious and worrisome, but agreeable, happy, and profitable, so that "our disposition [becomes] more congenial and pleasant" as a result of it. This is a refining influence of which Gellius would most certainly approve.

Fronto gives an insight into one detail of such a conversation in a letter to Marcus Aurelius, when he insists that great care must be taken to soften speech of any kind to prevent its becoming rough and rustic.[9] He goes on to suggest one of the means by which this may be accomplished when he recommends the retention of certain conventional artificialities (*artificia*) which had become part of speaking, both formal and informal alike.

As an example of what he means he cites Socrates and his methods, pointing to the fact that the philosopher never approached a subject or a fellow-conversationalist too directly but mounted a slow and careful attack, since it was his opinion that a man could be influenced only by a gracious and easy-going discussion. In other words, serious, unmasked criticism is not as effective as courtesy and consideration. It is hardly necessary to point yet again to the fact that Socrates and his methods are constantly being related to urbanity, especially as it appears in conversation.

It is perhaps worth looking at an example of impolite conversation by way of contrast. Early in his collection (1.2.4) Gellius begins to describe what should be a pleasant, congenial dinner at the villa of Herodes Atticus just outside Athens. When the guests sit back to enjoy the usual after-dinner conversation, however, a young Stoic begins prattling on "unceasingly in a perverse and fatuous manner" in praise of his philosophy, even going to the extreme of labeling all other Greek and Roman authorities as "rough and rustic." The author may intend a subtle irony in the adjectives here, since they would better apply to the young man and his not very edifying diatribe than to his opponents.

Although the evidence is sparse, it is also clear that an interest in proper accent and intonation still exists. At first sight, Fronto's description of a stutterer may seem to have little connection with such subtleties of speech, but a glance at the list of adjectives which the author uses to describe this shortcoming and normal speech which is its counterpart makes it clear that, as in earlier times, dissonance (*vox absona*) is balanced against a smooth tone of voice (*vox lenis*).[10]

Spartianus' description of Hadrian's abortive attempt to speak before the senate when he was quaestor suggests that the cultured urban accent was also much respected,[11] for, though he does not go into detail, he does say that the future emperor was laughed at because he recited "in a rather rustic fashion." Many faults may be included in the criticism, but it is highly likely that a provincial accent overshadowed everything else.[12] The reaction of the senate and the fact that Hadrian took it to heart shows that the shortcoming is as unacceptable as ever.

But this is only half the truth, for an episode in the *Noctes Atticae* (19.9) shows that complications have set in. Once again Gellius begins describing a dinner party that has good promise of being sophisticated and successful, but it is not long before the conversation takes a nasty turn as several Greeks accost the rhetorician Julianus with being "a barbarian and a rustic." They give two reasons for feeling this way: not only is Julianus a Spaniard, but he also works with the Latin language. Cicero would take quick exception to the second element of their criticism, of course, but he would probably join with them on the first count, for their gibe is directed, at least in part, at Julianus' Spanish accent (2), which is apparently the same fault that the orator could not abide in Sextilius Ena and the other poets of Corduba. But the contrast between Cicero's attitude and Gellius' is striking, for the later writer is not at all bothered by the Spanish flavor of Julianus' speech. He insists that the rhetorician has a high reputation in Rome (2) and all but applauds him as he defends Latin as his native tongue (8) and equates himself with "the Latin name" (9). There can be little doubt that a change in attitude regarding the purity of accent has taken place as Rome has become more cosmopolitan.

A glance at the *Scriptores Historiae Augustae* of the third and fourth centuries shows further indications of a dilution or leveling of urbanity. First there is the fact that *urbanus* and *urbanitas* seem to have moved completely away from denoting anything exclusively Roman. When the leader of the Dalmatians, for example, is described by Trebellius Pollio as helping the Gallieni "very courteously and very wisely,"[13] *urbanus* can only denote refinement in the broadest possible sense. In a passage of Flavius Vopiscus the precise meaning and application of *urbanitas* are not entirely clear, but the writer seemingly means to say that Probus "entered the territory of the barbarians . . . either by instilling fear in them or by taking advantage of their willingness to receive him" (*urbanitate*).[14] If this is a fair interpretation of Vopiscus' meaning, then the abstract seems to have become a form of courtesy and good will that even barbarians can exhibit. *Urbanitas* has fallen far, then, though it is no wonder that it is in this position when men like Maximinus are able to aspire to the highest office that the state has to offer.

If Lampridius may be believed, the Roman people, the senate, and even the provincials mourned the death of Severus, not only for the usual reasons but also because of the "roughness and rusticity of his successor Maximinus."[15] Elsewhere this creature is described as a savage, rough, half-barbarian shepherd who was actually labeled "a petty Thracian" by his contemporaries.[16] It is not difficult to imagine what was happening to contemporary refinement under such influences, though this is not to say that everyone aspiring to such a position was a barbarian. Clodius Albinus for one had lost all evidence of his foreign extraction. But it is significant and at the same time a little pathetic that, when this has happened, it is worth noting.[17]

Severus falls somewhere between Maximinus and Albinus, for he evidently had a pleasant voice, but retained an African accent throughout his life.[18] Even from this cursory glance, then, it may be concluded that the standards of urbanity which were threatening to disappear in the first century after Christ were largely lost by the third and fourth centuries, and shortcomings that were earlier rejected outright could now be accepted without qualm.

A search for an urbane man of the third or fourth century is largely unrewarding, for there is only one writer of the fourth century who even vaguely qualifies, and his refinement does not bear scrutiny. Symmachus who, among other things, wrote letters ostensibly in imitation of Pliny presents himself as a well-educated man of the time taking an active part in politics and searching for the refined leisure that so many writers before him had sought. He is perfectly well aware of the contrast between the hustle and bustle of the city and the relative peace and quiet of the country and shows a strong interest in the retreat offered by a spa like Baiae or by his country villa.

But it takes more than this to make a gentleman in the Roman sense, and a reading of Symmachus' letters soon reveals that he has no real interest in matters of sophistication. Not only is there seldom any show of urbane wit and little true appreciation of literature, but it is impossible, even anachronistic, to imagine Symmachus discussing and defending *urbanitas*. The Roman feeling has gone and so has the Roman gentleman. This is not surprising, for Rome and the Romans have become completely different from what they used to be and the special group in Rome which claimed *urbanitas* has largely disappeared. Moreover, there is no spirit of freedom and progress such as existed in Ciceronian and Augustan times and even under the better of the early emperors. True urbanity needs the optimism bred by a free, productive atmosphere.

To this point no mention has been made of the Christian writers, and perhaps it would be better to omit them, since it is an immense task merely to determine whether they deserve consideration. A few random observations, however, will be useful to show the kind of information that might be gleaned from them. At least one early Christian writer is able to identify an urbanity of speech, for Jerome characterized Isaiah as "a man well born, of urban speech, not having any rusticity in his expression."[19] But this in itself shows an extension in the application of the abstract, for Isaiah was hardly a Roman. The observation stands as an extreme example of the development that has already been noticed in the pagan writers of the century before.

Urbanitas is used once by Tertullian in his *Apologeticus* (21.30) in what appears to be an attempt to designate a true Roman urbanity as he asserts that Christ can lead men who are "highly civilized, yet deceived by their urbanity" (*expolitos et urbanitate deceptos*) to a realization of the truth. It is easy to see how the Christians might have objected to this sophistication, for it was a pagan tradition with its roots deep in the past and as such was an idea that was potentially difficult to combat and eradicate. That it had to be eradicated was perfectly obvious since concepts of refinement and sophistication were diametrically opposed to the simple, ascetic outlook of the early Christians.[20] If a reliable judgment may be based on a single occurrence, then it would appear that this view of *urbanitas* persisted through the sixth century, for Gregory describes it as a perverse attitude to things Christian.[21]

It was impossible, then, that amid the barbarizing of Rome and the gradual Christianizing of the pagan world *urbanitas*, which was so peculiarly Roman, could find a place on either side. One of two things happened to it as time passed: it was either rejected outright by thinkers like Tertullian or else the abstract came to signify a general, all-embracing refinement that accrued to a man living in a city—any city. Bonaventure in the thirteenth century used the word in this general sense[22] and so did Stow nearly four centuries later.[23] But it is a far cry from the urbanity of Cicero, Horace, and Pliny.

GREEK URBANITY
TO THE FIFTH CENTURY B.C.

It is important to note that in the *Iliad* and *Odyssey* there is evidence, tenuous and scattered though it may be, that the city and urban feelings are coming into being, though the fact that both πόλις and ἄστυ are used suggests that not even the designation of such centers is fixed.[1] Achilles observes at the games for Patroclus that he who wins the "shot put" will not have to send his shepherd or ploughman to town (πόλιν) for iron for a full five years (*Il.* 23.826–35). Here the metal suggests that Homer is dealing with his own time, and the city seems to be a source of supply. At the same time it is interesting to note a certain suspicion: one does not go there unless he really has to, and the dependence on the city is a grudging one.

The best description of the physical characteristics of the center of population in Homeric times is that of the two cities on the shield of Achilles (18.490–606). In the one that is first described, people are engaged in normal urban pursuits, among which the marriage procession in the streets and the trial in the agora with its eager throng of spectators stand out. The terminology is ambivalent. The city begins as a πόλις (490), but soon has become an ἄστυ (493). The second city, this one described as a πόλις, is a walled establishment set off from, but in close proximity to, the countryside. If the two descriptions are put together, it is possible to conclude with Mumford that "by the eighth century, possibly, the Greek city had begun to acquire a physiognomy of its own,"[2] for here there are three of the most important physical constituents of the city state: the wall, the agora, and the population.[3]

The *Odyssey* offers slightly better evidence, since Ithaca is the scene of action in the later books. At times it is identified as an ἄστυ, but most often it is described as a πόλις. Whatever its designation, it is the center of population and activity. Because of the wealth and population concentrated here, beggars find that success comes easiest when they beg in the city (17.18f.); it is to Ithaca that the ship naturally makes its way after dropping Telemachus on his farm (16.330f.). After he has preceded Eumaeus and Odysseus to town, Telemachus is caught sight of making his way to the market place (17.52, 61–73). But in spite of such scattered references, and in spite of the reader's being constantly aware of Ithaca's existence in the latter part of the *Odyssey*, the city eludes detailed description.

One of the strongest arguments in favor of at least the partial development of the city by Homer's time lies in the contrast between it as the center of population and the country or fields nearby. This is evident in Achilles' speech mentioned above and in the description of the second city on the shield of Achilles. It is perhaps most striking in the latter half of the *Odyssey* where the balance between Odysseus' Ithaca and the country land of Eumaeus and his cronies is not only developed naturally but is also made integral to the plot. The balance is carefully maintained: Eumaeus does not go to the city (πόλινδε) but stays with his swine (14.372ff.); Odysseus questions the swineherd to see if he will let him stay at the farm or will send him to the city (πόλινδε: 15.305f.); Telemachus tells his men to go to town (ἀστύδε), while he goes to visit his fields (ἀγρούς: 15.503f.); the beggar already mentioned above has better luck in the city (κατὰ πτόλιν) than in the country (κατ' ἀγρούς) where he has to work for his keep (17.18f.); Eumaeus and Odysseus go from the country (ἐξ ἀγροῖο) to the city (πόλινδε: 17.182f.). There is also the formula ἐπ' ἀγροῦ νόσφι πόληος which cannot be pressed, but which at least shows the separation.[4] Elsewhere in the *Odyssey* the same separation of city and country is evident when Laertes in Odysseus' absence prefers to remain in the country (ἀγρῷ) and does not go to town (πόλινδε: 11.187f.). Slightly different is a mention of those living in the city and those dwelling around it (8.550f.).

By now it has become apparent that far more frequent and explicit reference to the contrast between city and country is to be found in the *Odyssey* than in the *Iliad*. There may be any number of reasons for this difference, not the least being that of subject matter. But a glance at the vocabulary used suggests another reason. Ἀγρός in the *Odyssey* is a fairly standard word for the country and its fields, while it occurs only twice in the *Iliad*—once in the speech of Achilles, in a line in which, as Leaf has pointed out, there is a decided "Odyssean reminiscence,"[5] and once in a simile drawn from country life (5.137). This difference at least suggests that in the *Odyssey* there exists a clearer identification of the country as opposed to the center of population. But care must be taken not to imagine the city as being better developed than it is. The picture of the townspeople gathered about the fountain outside the town (*Od.* 17.204–207), together with that of the sheep coming into town at dusk (17.170–73), suggests that the center still retains many of its rustic characteristics.

Since city and country are in the process of developing separate identities, it would be natural to expect a concomitant evolution in attitudes. Certainly Achilles' speech mentioned above suggests that the man living in the country was not strongly drawn towards the town. Moreover, in the description of the shield of Achilles, though an appreciation of both rustic and urban life is presented, the praise of the country makes it as attractive as or even more attractive than its counterpart.[6]

But what about the other side of the coin? Is there any evidence for a city pride and refinement which might be taken as constituting an urbanity? Although the evidence is sparse, the answer to this question must be in the affirmative, for twice in the *Odyssey* such a refinement is given expression. When Eumaeus and Odysseus meet Melantheus in the vivid scene at the fountain (17.204–53), the goatherd in his prideful, swaggering way expresses thorough contempt for these two of low station. Throughout his tirade he betrays a consciousness of social position, although it is difficult to see how he justifies feeling this way. If what Eumaeus says after the outburst is true (244ff.), then it may be logical to conclude that Melantheus has fallen prey to the influence of the city. The town with its society would appear to be having its influence beyond its physical limits. The antagonism between Melantheus and Eumaeus is the antagonism between urbanite and rustic that was later to become a serious social problem. But this is not to say that Melantheus is a representative of the city. He is no urbane gentleman. Except for his attitude of superiority, there is little about him that suggests the city. He is still a rustic but one of the large group of country people that were undergoing a change in outlook under the spreading influence of the town.

This encounter with Melantheus provides a preview of the kind of treatment that Eumaeus and Odysseus will receive when they get to the palace. In the matter of details, Melantheus' warning (230ff.) is a clear anticipation of Antinous' hurling the footstool at Odysseus (462f.). Even though he is an extreme case, Antinous lashes out at the hero and his ilk for thus reminding Penelope of her misery. Presumably a man of the city would control his emotions, but these men are just "stupid rustics thinking only of the immediate" (21.85). Here is the first clear statement in ancient literature of the contempt of the city-dweller for the simple rustic. Already the countryman is typed as a rough, uneducated, unrefined boor.[7]

One more point must be made about the attitude which Antinous exhibits here. It is primarily that of an aristocrat. His refinement is an urbanity if the latter is taken to be a feeling or attitude that exists in the city or town and not necessarily one that arises out of or because of urban life. Stanford has suggested that Antinous' criticism is that of a townsman for a countryman.[8] This is only partially true. Ribbeck is much more accurate when he points to it as the contempt of a squire for a limited farmer.[9] By this reasoning, then, it becomes an expression of a developing urbanity springing from the developing city.

With the seventh century, the city emerges full blown from the semidarkness of Homeric times. It has become the center of life and activity that was promised by the *Iliad* and *Odyssey*. As the population became concentrated, people became more aware of one another, and so there developed a new consciousness of the importance of the individual and an interest in his relationship to the larger life of the city. Now there arises a new and strong sense of patriotism perhaps best exemplified by Tyrtaeus' songs in praise of Sparta in which he urges his fellow citizens on to important undertakings.[10] Alcaeus a little later wrote his *Hymn to Mytilene* which, fragmentary though it may be, shows his attachment to his city.[11]

Along with this new sense of patriotism comes a careful analysis of the relationship between man and his city, an analysis that must have had its beginnings in the previous century. Alcaeus asserts that it is not buildings, walls, dock facilities, and the like that constitute a city, but men able, and presumably willing, to make use of opportunity.[12] It is the first recognition of the fact that cities reflect the personality of their inhabitants. But along with the opportunities which communal life has to offer come certain burdensome responsibilities. The men of Alcaeus' city are, for instance, its tower of defense in time of war.[13] It is most important to recognize the fact that in both of these fragments men have taken the place of the physical surroundings of the city. In both cases, whether it be for the enjoyment of opportunity or for carrying out the responsibilities of city life, man and the city are one. Their purposes and personalities are blended completely.

This evolution of the city also caused re-examination of time-honored relationships between individuals. From Theognis comes the complaint of the aristocrat who finds it extremely difficult to accept the fact that the good old days of the aristocracy are gone.[14] There is a trace of Antinous' disdain for the "stupid rustics" in Theognis' lament that, while the city may be the same physically, the people are rustic, uncouth outsiders who ". . . are now the honored (ἀγαθοί) . . . while those who earlier were the nobles are now the low."[15]

The city-dweller now becomes aware also of the foreigner and the influence he is having. Xenophanes lashes out at the Lydians from whom the people of Colophon are "learning useless refinements" and then proceeds to a vivid description.[16] Anacreon, about the same time, discloses that he has no use for the Sintians and Scythians[17] and attacks a certain Artemon who, in spite of the fact that he was once an uncouth Cimmerian, has risen to a position of wealth and power in the city.[18]

Thus, in the seventh and sixth centuries before Christ, man has become completely aware of his city and the special flavor of its society. As in Homeric times, there is much that is still aristocratic in this feeling of superiority. But the context is now the fully developed city. The attitude comes as much from an analysis of a man's relationship to others within and without the city as it does from the aristocratic tradition. And so this sense of refinement or exclusiveness may be called a true urbanity.

Articulation of urbanity is not frequent in these two centuries, mainly because the sources are so fragmentary. Alcman makes the first clear statement: "You are not a rustic nor are you some clumsy, stupid person, nor a Thessalian, nor an Erysichean, nor a shepherd, but a man from lofty Sardes."[19] Interpretation of this passage for the present purposes must be qualified not only by the textual problems, but by the fact that Alcman more likely than not is a native of Sardes and that this city is not as purely Greek as it might be. But the fact remains that here, about the middle of the seventh century, there exists a clear statement in which the inhabitant of a substantial city is set off as superior to the clumsy rustic and rude barbarian.

A little later Sappho lashes out at Andromeda for her attentions to a rustic wench (ἀγροίωτις) who does not even know that she should keep her ankles covered.[20] At first sight the criticism may seem petty, but its significance becomes clearer if we remember that such negligence is often criticized in Greek and Latin literature.[21] Whether it is petty or not, it is important, first because it shows once again very clearly that the city-dweller is aware of his refinement and secondly because it gives an insight into what constitutes this refinement, at least in one detail.[22]

What happens to an urbanite when he is forced to give up his city and experience the rustic outer world for an extended period of time is the subject of a fragment of Alcaeus.[23] Here the aristocratic urbanite shouts out from exile in longing for his position in the city. His desire to hear the assembly is a manifestation of his missing the cultural company and the other refinements that the city has to offer.[24] But more striking is the impression that rusticity has made on him. He has been experiencing, not another way of life, but a fate (μοῖρα: Dare we call it a form of doom?) which had to be endured and which has left the poet thoroughly miserable (τάλαις). In this intensely personal outpouring of emotion it is possible to see how great the rift was between city and country in the late seventh or early sixth century B.C. Alcaeus' remark recalls a fragment of Phocylides from about the middle of the century in which he expresses his preference for living in the heart of the city.[25]

A line from a poem of Simonides provides a final comment on these centuries. With his assertion that "a city teaches a man"[26] comes recognition of an important fact that lies behind the sentiments already discussed. Whether it be a village, town, or full-fledged city, and whether the education be rudimentary, elementary, or highly sophisticated, the center of population is the place of dissemination of knowledge. By Simonides' time, this fact was clearly recognized. It is possible to go a step further in interpreting the remark and see in it a stage in the development of an idea that culminated in Pericles' lofty ideal of Athens as the educative center for the whole of Greece.

THE STOIC *Urbanitas*

In a letter to Appius Claudius Pulcher written in 50 B.C., Cicero presents what at first sight appears to be a unique and perplexing use of *urbanitas*.[1] After describing Appius as a man who possesses great wisdom (*summa prudentia*), much formal learning (*multa ... doctrina*), and a vast practical experience (*plurimo rerum usu*), he goes on to: *addo urbanitatem quae est virtus ut Stoici rectissime putant.* Lammermann relates the noun here to the Stoic ἀστεῖος, apparently equating it with σπουδαῖος and ἀγαθός,[2] and goes on to suggest Panaetius as a direct connection between the Greek and Roman concepts through his discussion of urbanity and the urbane man in *De Officiis* (1.133f.). Lutsch, on the other hand, has no trouble seeing *urbanitas* as equaling *iustitia* or what he calls *Rechtsgefühl*.[3] There may be a grain of truth in both of these interpretations, but it is difficult to see how the one can get "the good" out of *urbanitas*, and how the other can find "justice" in it, since in no other context does the abstract seem to have such connotations.

It is perhaps better to start from Tyrrell and Purser's notion that *urbanitas* here denotes "politeness" and to recognize the fact, as they do, that it can be a *virtus* simply because the Stoics had any number of virtues above and beyond the cardinal ones.[4] There is confirmation of this idea in one important passage of the *De Officiis* (3.20–25) where Cicero is presenting a discussion of justice. Because he is undoubtedly following a Stoic source, it may be assumed with some confidence that his statement of principle (24) has this origin: *multo magis est secundum naturam excelsitas animi et magnitudo itemque comitas, iustitia, liberalitas quam voluptas, quam vita, quam divitiae.* The key word, of course, is *comitas,* which on a number of occasions has been related to urbanity[5] and which stands here beside fairness (*iustitia*) and generosity (*liberalitas*) as one of the more admirable human characteristics. The company that it keeps in this passage makes it clear that it is in essence a virtue, even though it is not designated as such. It is not surprising to find such respect for refinement when one remembers that in Book One of the *De Officiis,* Panaetius-Cicero develops a strong connection between the *urbanus homo* and the principle of decorum which Panaetius called τὸ πρέπον.[6]

ABBREVIATIONS

AJP: *American Journal of Philology.*

Bergk: Bergk, Th. *Poetae Lyrici Graeci*⁴. 3 vols. Teubner, 1878–82.

CJ: *Classical Journal.*

CP: *Classical Philology.*

CQ: *Classical Quarterly.*

CR: *Classical Review.*

CW: *Classical World.*

FAC: Edmonds, J. M. *The Fragments of Attic Comedy.* 3 vols. Leiden, 1957–61.

FCG: Meineke, A. *Fragmenta Comicorum Graecorum.* 5 vols. Berlin, 1839–57.

HSCP: *Harvard Studies in Classical Philology.*

Jahresb: *Jahresbericht über die Fortschritte der klassischen Altertumswissenschaft.*

LCL: *Loeb Classical Library.*

LG: Edmonds, J. M. *Lyra Graeca.* (*LCL*). 3 vols. London, 1922–31.

Lobel-Page: Lobel, E., and D. Page. *Poetarum Lesbiorum Fragmenta.* Oxford, 1955.

OCT: *Oxford Classical Text.*

ORF: Malcovati, E. *Oratorum Romanorum Fragmenta*². 3 vols. Turin, 1955.

RE: Pauly-Wissowa, *Real-Encyclopädie der classischen Altertumswissenschaft.*

REL: *Revue des études latines.*

ROL: Warmington, E. H. *Remains of Old Latin.* (*LCL*). 4 vols. Cambridge (Mass.) and London, 1935–40.

Schanz-Hosius: Schanz, Martin. *Geschichte der römischen Literatur,* rev. by Carl Hosius. vols. 1 and 2 (*Handbuch der Altertumswissenschaft Abt.* 8, *Teil* 1 and 2). Munich, 1927 and 1935.

SRP: Ribbeck, Otto. *Scaenicae Romanorum Poesis Fragmenta³.* 2 vols. Leipzig, 1897–98.

TAPA: *Transactions and Proceedings of the American Philological Association.*

Walde-Hofmann: Walde, A. *Lateinisches etymologisches Wörterbuch⁴,* rev. by J. B. Hofmann. 2 vols. Heidelberg, 1965.

NOTES

INTRODUCTION

1. *The City in History*, 398.
2. 15 ff., 175 f.

CHAPTER I

GREEK URBANITY IN THE CLASSICAL PERIOD AND AFTER

1. It is not necessary for the present purposes to go into the question of whether the speech is actually that given by Pericles or whether it is largely a creation of Thucydides. The truth probably lies somewhere between these extremes.

2. *Ach.* 370–73; *Peace* 632–48. An interesting statement involving urbanity appears in the form of a recommendation made by Isocrates to Nicocles the young ruler of Cyprus: ἀστεῖος εἶναι πειρῶ καὶ σεμνός· τὸ μὲν γὰρ τῇ τυραννίδι πρέπει, τὸ δὲ πρὸς τὰς συνουσίας ἁρμόττει (*To Nicocles* 34). It would appear that the author is recommending an outward reserve which must be balanced by a depth of culture and refinement, a combination which will enable the ruler not only to exhibit the dignity and aloofness that suit a man in his position, but to approach others in an affable, refined way without losing his dignity. This seems to be the same sense of decorum and restraint, cultured outlook, generosity, and feeling of consideration for one's fellow citizen that appear in the funeral speech.

3. Cf. Thuc., *Hist.* 2.13, 94. Plato, *Rep.* 1.327A, 328C; *Symp.* 172A. Demosth., *Against Lept.* 12.

4. Aesch., *Eum.* 997; *Supp.* 501, 618.

5. The discussion of Socrates which follows is for the most part a summary of the conclusions reached by Karl Lammermann in his *Von der*

attischen Urbanität und ihrer Auswirkung in der Sprache, 26–82. This is the only study of Greek urbanity that has been done, and, except for an introductory chapter, it is limited to Plato's Socrates.

6. In Xenophon's *Cyropedia* (2.2.12) there is a reference to this urbane wit. The man of refinement is not out to harm anyone with his witticisms, for he is above making petty attacks on his fellow man and is not seeking personal gain. His primary purpose is to offer enjoyment. The adjective ἀστεῖον is used a number of times in connection with this urbane wit: Aristoph., *Wasps* 1258; Aristot., *Rhet.* 3.10 (1410b). Aristotle speaks of ἀστειολογίαι in *Rhet. Alex.* 1436a. By Demetrius' time ἀστεϊσμός had been adopted to refer to humor in general. Cf. *Peri Herm.* 128 ff. and Grube's note on this in his *A Greek Critic: Demetrius on Style,* 135f. W. Rhys Roberts' note in the glossary of his *Demetrius on Style* (Cambridge, 1902), 269f. is also worth reading.

7. Fr. 685 (*OCT*).

8. Isoc., *Antid.* 296. Cic., *De Or.* 3.42ff. On the passage of Isocrates see G. Norlin, *Isocrates* (London, 1929) (*LCL*), 2, 348f., n. "d," where the translator suggests that the Attic dialect was the least provincial, whereas the Doric was harsh and the Ionic soft and effeminate. The passage from Cicero is discussed below, page 60. Perhaps it was an awareness of the urban mode of speaking that enabled Aristophanes to call Cleophon a shrieking Thracian (*Frogs* 678–82) and caused the populace to despise Stephanus the Acharnian (Demosth., *Against Steph.* 1.1110.30).

9. I have attempted to deal with Menander's discussion of the problems and the solution he offers in my "City and Country in Menander's *Dyskolos,*" *Philologus* 110 (1966), 194–211. Most of what follows is a summary of what I have said there.

10. On the cook, see Theoph., *Char.* 6.

11. There is no time here to analyze the ἄγροικος and his ἀγροικία. Otto Ribbeck has done a good job of describing such matters in his *Agroikos, eine ethologische Studie.* See also the many references to the rustic and his life in W. E. Heitland, *Agricola, A Study of Agriculture and Rustic Life in the Greco-Roman World from the Point of View of Labour,* 16–130. Theophrastus gives a brief but perceptive picture of the rustic (*Char.* 4).

12. *Clouds* 491f., 628f., 646. Cf. *Knights* 808.

13. *Knights* 315–18; *Peace* 632–48. Cf. *Ach.* 370–73.

14. Heliod., *Aethiop.* 7.10.3.

15. 1.8.9. There is a similar use of ἄμορφος at 6.7.1 where it is used with ἄγροικος to describe ugliness.

16. In Theocritus' *Idyll* 20.1–10 the sophisticated Eunica ridicules the

166

countryman for his shaggy look, his uncouth way of talking, and his rough games.

CHAPTER II
EARLY ROMAN URBANITY

1. F. Leo, *Geschichte der römischen Literatur* (Berlin, 1913), 11.

2. Thelma B. De Graff (*Naevian Studies*, 51) seems to take this passage at face value.

3. Enzo V. Marmorale (*Naevius Poeta*, 221) translates these words *lepidamente e mordacemente*.

4. Unfortunately, it is impossible to know when the words first appeared in Latin or how they developed semantically. If, as Ribbeck and others believe, they are derived from the Greek, then they may have been adopted from southern Italy or Sicily. If, as seems more likely, *scurra* comes from the Etruscan, it may represent one more refining influence from that direction. On the derivation of *facetus* see Ribbeck, *Agroikos*, 55 and Walde-Hofmann 1, 438f. On the derivation of *scurra* see Ribbeck, 64ff.; *RE*, art. *scurra*, 2 reihe, vol. 3, 911f. (Hug); Walde-Hofmann 2, 502f.

5. J. H. Waszink, "Tradition and Personal Achievement in Early Latin Literature," *Mnemosyne*, 4 ser., 13 (1960), 21.

6. It is tempting to relate these to Aristotle's ἀστειολογίαι (*Rhet. Alex.* 1436a).

7. 741. This contrast between Athenian and foreigner occurs again in the *Mercator* (633ff.) and the *Stichus* (669ff.) where Attic citizens are set against *peregrini*. Such statements surely helped reinforce similar feelings at Rome. Parallel in thought, though by no means as clearly stated, is Lampadio's jab at the Lydians (*Cist.* 559–63).

8. *Sat.* 3.58–125.

9. Quoted by Cicero (*Or.* 152): *quam nunquam vobis Grai atque barbari.*

10. Quoted by Nonius (1.10): *quid narras, barbare cum indomitis moribus,/inlitterate? inlex es.* Plautus uses the word in the same way in the *Bacchides* (121, 123) where it describes Lydus' stupidity.

11. Elsewhere, the adjective and its cognates are used to designate what is Italian: *Capt.* 492, 884; *Cas.* 748; *Curc.* 150; *Mil. Glor.* 211; *Most.* 828; *Poen.* 598; *Stich.* 193. On the passages from the *Captivi* see W. M. Lindsay, *The Captivi of Plautus* (London, 1900), n. ad l.884, p. 319. On the *Miles Gloriosus* see R. Y. Tyrrell, *The Miles Gloriosus of T. Maccius Plautus* (London, 1899), n. ad l.212, p. 159.

There is surely little purpose in speculating as to where this humorous use of *barbarus* originated. A note of E. W. Fay in his edition of the *Mostellaria* (Boston, 1902), n. *ad* l.828, pp. 131 f., shows how futile such speculation can be. It is perhaps better to take Chalmers' point of view: "The frequency of his jocular references to the Romans as *barbari* or *pultiphagi* indicates that this was a popular jest and that his audiences had enough sense of humour to appreciate a joke directed against themselves." ("Plautus and His Audience," in *Roman Drama* [ed. by T. A. Dorey and Donald R. Dudley], 25.)

12. It is mentioned by Festus (174, Lindsay) who quotes the only extant line: *Virgo sum; nondum didici nupta verba dicere.* It is interesting that Cnemon's daughter who is the only one in the Greek play that could have made this statement has nothing like this to say.

13. On the *Astiologa* see *SRP* 2, 10. Ribbeck (*Agroikos*, 46 f.) connects this title and presumably the theme of the play with Aristotle's ἀστεῖα (*Rhet.* 3.10[1410b]). Schanz-Hosius (1, 51) list this title among Naevius' comedies. Edmonds (*FAC* 3, 1214), following Ribbeck, lists the *Astiologa* of Naevius as coming possibly from a Greek original Ἡ Ἀστειόλογος. The Latin title he translates "The Witty Wench," though it is difficult to see how that can be garbled out of Nonius' corruption.

14. Nonius (258 f.): *'Contendere' significat comparare ... Caecilius Titthe*: *Egon vitam meam/Atticam contendam cum istac rusticana Syra?*

15. Charinus in his opening monologue of the *Mercator* (61–72) outlines a similar contrast.

16. 269: *Rus merum hoc quidemst.* This passage calls to mind Ampelisca's reprimand directed at Sceparnio in the *Rudens* (424). As he tries to take liberties with her, she brushes him off with *non ego sum pollucta pago: potin ut me abstineas manum?*

17. Cf. Chalmers, "Plautus and His Audience," 24.

18. Cf. *Truc.* 655, where the *urbs* is ostensibly Athens but could also suggest Rome to Plautus' audience.

19. Two instances of *agrestis* in the fragments of Pacuvius show extended meanings. In the *Periboea* (*ROL* 2, 276 [ll.297f.] *agrestia* is coupled with *ardua* to describe certain *loca.* Presumably the physical roughness of these places is implied in the adjectives. If so, this is a unique metaphoric application of *agrestis.* The second instance involves a fragment of the *Antiopa* where a tortoise in a riddle is described as *quadrupes tardigrada, agrestis, humilis ... (ROL* 2, 160 [ll.4ff.]). Perhaps the adjective merely designates the turtle as a creature living in the fields, but it is equally possible that Pacuvius is using the word to underline the general impression that this slow-moving, ugly, and rather dull-witted creature leaves. Some of the roughness and

168

grotesqueness of the instance in the *Periboea* may be among the connotations of the adjective here.

20. On *urbanus* in this early period see Ferdinand Heerdegen, *De vocabuli quod est urbanus apud vetustiores scriptores Latinos vi atque usu.*

21. Eduard Fraenkel (*Plautinisches im Plautus*, 187–97) has argued that, even though there are elements of a structure that could reflect a Greek original, the *rex-regina* (Jupiter-Juno) doublet is a purely Roman combination.

22. Worth a mention in passing is the occurrence of *scurra* in the *Curculio* (296f.). Leo (*Geschichte der römischen Literatur*, 142, 146) and Fraenkel (*Plautinisches im Plautus*, 130f.) believe this is a picture from the streets of Rome. Jean Collart (*T. Maccius Plautus Curculio. Plaute, Charançon* [Paris, 1962], 63), in his note on ll.285f., leaves the possibility open that the playwright is following his model here. The *scurrae* in *Poen.* 612 would also be Roman if Fraenkel is right in suggesting that this line is Plautine in spirit (42). It is equally difficult to know what Plautus intends when he uses the term in *Epid.* 15 and *Poen.* 1280f. Fraenkel (18f.) has pointed to Plautine characteristics in lines preceding and following the example in the *Poenulus* (1271ff. and 1289ff.). In the *Truculentus* the mention of "Attic Athens" (497) gives *scurra* which has occurred a few lines earlier (491) the connotation of Greek urbanity.

23. Ribbeck (*Agroikos*, 55) seems to feel that this is a group that is new in influence. Referring to this passage of the *Trinummus* (199–202), he calls these *scurrae* a "... *neue Klasse geschäftiger Neuigkeitskrämer*."

24. Pliny, *N.H.* 29.14.

25. *Bacch.* 743; *Most.* 22, 64; *Truc.* 87. There is little else in early literature to indicate how the gentleman felt about other non-Italian foreigners. Two comments of Cato touch upon the subject. The Ligurians are described by him as being treacherous (*fallaces, insidiosi*), ignorant (*inlitterati*), and lying (*mendaces*) (Serv., *ad Aen.* 11.700, 715), while elsewhere he says that they are consistent in the pursuit of two things, the military life and sly talking (Charisius 263 [Barwick]). These comments are not very satisfying and stem as much from philosophic and patriotic feelings as from any sense of urbanity.

26. J. Wight Duff, *A Literary History of Rome from the Origins to the Close of the Golden Age*[3] (ed. by A. M. Duff) (London, 1953), 96 and n. 4.

27. *Mil. Glor.* 648. In *Cas.* 67–74 and *Rud.* 631 Plautus once again appears to be poking fun at these people. On the latter passage see Chalmers, "Plautus and His Audience," 46.

28. *SRP* 2, 9f. (from Macrobius, *Sat.* 3.18.6): (A) *Quis heri/apud te?*

(B) *Praenestini et Lanuvini hospites./* (A) *Suopte utrosque decuit acceptos cibo,/ altris inanem volvulam madidam dari,/ altris nuces in proclivi profundier.* The nuts of Praeneste were evidently famous in ancient times. See Marmorale, *Naevius Poeta*, n. *ad loc.*, pp. 208f.

29. *Bacch.* 12. Speaking of this passage, Chalmers ("Plautus and His Audience," 46) says that Praeneste was probably one of Rome's more important neighbors and that this comment of Plautus may be just a time-honored "joke based on inter-city rivalry." But he mentions the fact that a feeling of cultural superiority on the part of the Romans is implied.

30. 493 (Lindsay): *Tammodo antiqui dicebant pro modo.*

31. Th. Bergk (*Kleine philologische Schriften* [ed. by R. Peppmüller], I, 187f.) has interpreted *conia* and *rabo* in this way. Cf. E. S. Ramage, "Early Roman Urbanity," *AJP* 81 (1960), 69f. and note 15 there.

32. *Annales* 234–51 (Vahlen), quoted by Aul. Gell., *N. A.* 12.4.4. On this passage see Ulrich Knoche, "Über die Aneignung griechischer Poesie im älteren Rom," *Gymnasium* 65 (1958), 338 and O. Skutsch, "Enniana V," *CQ* 57 (1963), 94ff.

CHAPTER III
THE SCIPIONIC PERIOD

1. Hor., *Sat.* 1.4.1–8.

2. Cic., *Tusc.* 2.62; *Qu. Fr.* 1.1.23. Cf. George C. Fiske, *Lucilius and Horace*, 83, and H. J. Rose, *A Handbook of Latin Literature*[3] (New York, 1960), 98f.

3. Fiske, *Lucilius and Horace*, 83.

4. *Ibid.*, 72.

5. Cicero calls it *quoddam decorum* which is a translation of Panaetius' τὸ πρέπον. Modestus van Straaten (*Panétius, sa vie, ses écrits et sa doctrine avec une édition des fragments*, 282f.) expresses the opinion that, except for the references to things Roman, the first two books of Cicero's *De Officiis* represent a faithful account of Panaetius' doctrines. This is perhaps the safest stance to take.

6. Van Straaten (*Panétius*, 360–63) includes *De Off.* 1.93–101 as fragment 107 of Panaetius.

7. Fiske, *Lucilius and Horace*, 85ff.

8. John F. D'Alton, *Roman Literary Theory and Criticism*, 24.

9. Cf. Roy C. Flickinger, "Terence and Menander," *CJ* 26 (1930), 682–94.

10. 586–93. Cf. *Hec.* 613. In *Heaut.* 61–70, Chremes has almost the same reaction to the exile at hard labor that Menedemus has imposed on himself.

11. *Ad.* 42–46.

12. Quoted by Otto Rieth in *Die Kunst Menanders in den "Adelphen" des Terenz*, 25, who goes on to paraphrase: *Terenz hat die bäurisch derben Züge im Wesen Demeas verstärkt.*

13. Ἀδελφοί fr. 11 (Koerte 2, 19).

14. Rieth (*Die Kunst Menanders in den "Adelphen" des Terenz*, 115) leaves the impression that he does not consider that there is a significant difference in meaning between these lines: *Hier gibt Terenz den Sinn und die Weise Menanders genau wieder.*

15. 440 ff. *Ibid.*, 72.

16. *Ibid.*, 131.

17. *Ibid.*, 121, 131.

18. Hazel M. Toliver ("The Terentian Doctrine of Education," *CW* 43 [1949], 195–200) has discussed the apparent compromise reached at the end of the *Adelphoe.*

Not only the characters, but also the actions of Cnemon and Demea present strong points of comparison. Both must learn from experience, but neither changes completely. At the end of the play Demea still puts sternness first (*Ad.* 994), while Cnemon cannot completely overcome his misanthropy (cf. Ramage, "City and Country in Menander's *Dyskolos*," *Philologus* 110 [1966], 210). Konrad Gaiser in his comments appended to Rieth's book (*Die Kunst Menanders in den "Adelphen" des Terenz*, 149) points to the similarity between Demea's change and that of Cnemon: . . . *beide neigen zu übertriebener Strenge und sehen nach einem erschütternden Erlebnis das Verfehlte ihrer bisherigen Lebensweise ein, ohne zu einer wirklichen inneren Umkehr fähig zu sein.*

19. F. Marx, *C. Lucilii Carminum Reliquiae* (Leipzig, 1904–1905), 1, 8 (ll.88–94); *ROL* 3, 30 (ll.87–93). Hereafter reference will be made to these editions by affixing *M* or *W* to the line numbers (e.g., this Albucius fragment is 88–94M or 87–93W). Where the references are the same, they will be designated by *M* alone. On this fragment see Marx' comments, 2, 41–44. See also L. Müller, *Leben und Werke des Gaius Lucilius*, 42, and E. Grassi, "Nota a Lucilio," *Atene e Roma*, m.s., 6 (1961), 148. In the *Brutus* (131) Cicero calls Albucius *Doctus etiam Graecis . . . vel potius plane Graecus* and brushes him off as having no talent for oratory.

20. William Korfmacher, " 'Grecizing' in Lucilian Satire," *CJ* 30 (1934), 454.

21. *Sat.* 3.14.6 (*ORF* frag. 30, p. 133). Another fragment preserved by Gellius (6.12.1; *ORF* frag. 17, p. 127) points in this same direction.

22. Conrad Cichorius, *Untersuchungen zu Lucilius*, 227.

23. 497f.M, 540f.W. On this fragment see Marx, *C. Lucilii Carminum Reliquiae,* 2, 185f.

24. 166f.M, 159f.W.

25. 1063M, 1034W. Warmington reads *blennus,* while Marx prefers *plennus.* On the passage see Marx, *C. Lucilii Carminum Reliquiae,* 2, 338f.

26. 1067M, 1030W. Cf. *ROL* 3, 334f., n. "a".

27. 193M, 218W.

28. Cichorius (*Untersuchungen zu Lucilius,* 270) suggests that it is not a rustic feast that is under consideration at all, but that Lucilius is using *rusticus* in the extended sense of unpolished or rude. L. R. Shero ("Lucilius's *Cena Rustica,*" *AJP* 50 [1929], 66) says that Lucilius would not have ridiculed country food and imagines the satire to have been "a mock-heroic account of a country meal in which the humblest foods and simplest appointments would be described in grandiloquent terms, . . ." It is difficult to see how such an account would not involve some element of satire or ridicule, especially in the hands of Lucilius.

29. George C. Fiske, "The Plain Style in the Scipionic Circle" in *University of Wisconsin Studies in Language and Literature* 3 (Madison, 1919), 95. Cf. also his *Lucilius and Horace,* 139f., n. 106.

30. See below, page 109f.

31. Cichorius, *Untersuchungen zu Lucilius,* 16. On the passage of Cicero see below, page 60.

32. 1130M, 232W: *Cecilius pretor ne rusticus fiat.* On this line see Marx, *C. Lucilii Carminum Reliquiae,* 2, 358f.; Müller, *Leben und Werke des Gaius Lucilius,* 40; Cichorius, *Untersuchungen zu Lucilius,* 277f.; Ramage, "Early Roman Urbanity," *AJP* 81 (1960), 70f.

33. 210f.M, 233f.W.

34. There may be a hint of the same kind of criticism in another fragment where Pacilius is under discussion (581M, 623W). As I have tried to show elsewhere, however, ("Early Roman Urbanity," *AJP* 81 [1960], 71, n. 24) it is difficult to draw any conclusions about what Lucilius is trying to do here. There is also an interesting fragment of Titinius (104R): *Qui Obsce et Volsce fabulantur; nam Latine nesciunt.* Jules Marouzeau ("Plaute et la première 'crise du Latin'," *REL* 4 [1926], 103) says that Titinius . . . *raille ceux qui écrivent en latin osque et volsque*; . . . Schanz-Hosius (1, 142) have a slightly different view of the line: *Im Selbstgefühl des Lateiners spricht ein Togatendichter* (T. 104) *verächtlich sogar von den Leuten, welche oskisch und volskisch sprechen, da sie das Latein nicht kennen.* No matter which interpretation is accepted, the line shows that the Romans were thinking

about the relationship between Latin and the other languages. There is also perhaps a hint of an awareness of the superiority of Latin.

35. 963f.M, 983f.W. Fiske (*Lucilius and Horace*, 83) says pronunciation is under discussion here.

36. Cf. Cichorius, *Untersuchungen zu Lucilius*, 278.

37. There are a few other references to Italians that may or may not be important for present purposes. It is not clear what point Lucilius is making in his mention of the *scorta Pyrgensia* (1271M, 1178W). The satirist appears also to have lashed out at the Tusculans for their spite (1259M, 1132W), and there may be some contempt for the Samnites in his criticism of Aeserninus (149–52M, 172–75W), but it is unclear how far these feelings derive from his awareness of urbanity.

38. Duff (*A Literary History of Rome from the Origins to the Close of the Golden Age*, 156) has observed that Terence's style has an Attic grace and refinement, while Leo (*Geschichte der römischen Literatur*, 253) calls it a new Roman urbanity.

39. 615f.M, 710f.W. On these lines see Marx' comments (*C. Lucilii Carminum Reliquiae*, 2, 228f.).

40. *De Or.* 2.25.

41. In *Sat.* 1.10.65, he calls him *comis et urbanus* and at 1.4.7, he calls him *facetus*. He criticizes Lucilius' style in *Sat.* 1.4.9–13 and in 1.10.50f.

CHAPTER IV
THE CICERONIAN PERIOD

1. *Qu. Fr.* 3.1.6.

2. Much of what is said here about *urbanitas* is adapted from my article "*Urbanitas*: Cicero and Quintilian, a Contrast in Attitudes," *AJP* 84 (1963), 390–414. For discussion of previous studies and criticism of them see pp. 390f. and notes 13, 14, 22, 23, 29, 34, 38, 56.

3. *Carm.* 22.2 and 9.

4. *Fam.* 16.21.7.

5. *Fam.* 7.6.1: *desideria urbis et urbanitatis*; 7.17.1: *levis in urbis urbanitatisque desiderio*.

6. *Fam.* 7.31.2.

7. There is a similar combination in *De Or.* 2.40 where Crassus characterizes Antonius' orator as *inopem quendam humanitatis atque inurbanum*.

8. *De Nat. Deor.* 2.74. The idea that urbanity may transcend learning is hinted at elsewhere: *Fam.* 3.8.3; *De Or.* 1.72 and 2.25.

9. In *Fam.* 3.9.1, Cicero refers to Pulcher's regaining his politeness (*urbanitas*) after a period of strained relations between them.

10. *De Or.* 1.17. Cf. *Brut.* 177, where Caesar is described as excelling both in *festivitas* and *facetiae* and in *urbanitas, lepus,* and *suavitas.*

11. 1.159. This is surely one of the good qualities of the orator whom Cicero later describes as polished, learned, and urbane (*De Or.* 2.236).

12. In *De Fin.* 2.103, *homines* gives the term a broad connotation, while *urbanus* in *Att.* 12.6.4 has overtones of cleverness without an implication of Romanness.

13. *Fam.* 9.15.2: ... *Romani veteres et urbani sales; ego ... mirifice capior facetiis maxime nostratibus ....*

14. In *Fam.* 7.32.2, Cicero uses *urbanitas* once again to signify this cultured wit characteristic of the city-dweller. Here, too, there is a certain pessimism.

15. *De Fin.* 1.7. There is an apparent inconsistency between Cicero's statement here and his calling Lucilius *doctus et perurbanus* elsewhere (*De Or.* 1.72, 2.25). Presumably in these instances the emphasis is on cleverness and wit more than anything else.

16. Cicero admires this time-honored Roman wit in Marius along with that man's capacity for exhibiting extreme grace and elegance in his speech (*Qu. Fr.* 2.8.2). Lucius Licinius Crassus also had this gift (*De Or.* 2.228; *Brut.* 143).

17. *Inst. Orat.* 6.3.105f. G. L. Hendrickson ("Horace and Valerius Cato II," *CP* 12 [1917], 90ff.) asserts that this is Valerius Cato, although he admits that even Quintilian thought it to be Cato the Censor. I earlier took exception to his interpretation in my "Early Roman Urbanity," *AJP* 81 (1960), 70, n. 16, but I have since come around to his way of thinking. Cato's work with Lucilius' *Satires* and the fact of his being a neoteric poet would naturally involve such an interest. Lucilius had the reputation for being *doctus et perurbanus,* while urbanity and the *urbanus homo* were very much in the thoughts of neoteric poets such as Catullus. Charles Henderson, Jr., in his unpublished dissertation, "A Lexicon of the Stylistic Terms Used in Roman Literary Criticism," 1075, also leans toward Valerius Cato as the author of the definition.

18. *Carm.* 50.

19. *Att.* 1.16.10.

20. 170f. See Ramage, "Cicero on Extra-Roman Speech," *TAPA* 92 (1961), 486ff. and below, 71f. for further discussion of these orators.

21. ... *illud est maius, quod in vocibus nostrorum oratorum retinnit quiddam et resonat urbanius.*

22. The parallelism between this statement and that of *Brut.* 167, where Cicero mentions an Attic urbanity of wit, is worth noting.

23. *lenitate vocis atque ipso oris pressu et sono.* Cf. *De Or.* 2.182f., where

Cicero says that among other things a *lenitas vocis* is important for the successful orator. Catulus is mentioned twice again in the *Brutus* as being learned. At one point (259) Cicero says that it was his *suavitas vocis et lenis appellatio litterarum* more than his erudition that brought success, while in the other instance (133) Cicero says he was noted for the *sonus vocis* and his *suavitas appellandarum litterarum*.

24. It is worth remembering that the Roman populace was much more aware of sound in speech than we are nowadays. Cf. *De Or.* 3.196 and *Or.* 173.

25. I had already said this both in my dissertation and in my *"Urbanitas*: Cicero and Quintilian," *AJP* 84 (1963), 400ff., when Professor Carl Trahman drew my attention to the fact that Charles Henderson, Jr., had come to much the same conclusion some years earlier in his unpublished dissertation, "A Lexicon of the Stylistic Terms," 1073. Here he describes *urbanus* as "denoting the cultured pronunciation and vocal timbre of the city-dweller." This is probably what Cicero is referring to in the *Brutus* (239) when he calls Torquatus *toto genere perurbanus*.

26. *De Or.* 1.260f.

27. It is possible that Cicero has these ideas in mind when in the *Brutus* (227) he describes P. Antistius, who evidently was not a great orator, as having "a not inurbane appearance."

28. 133–37. As he begins this section on propriety in speech (132) the reader is struck by similarities between the vocabulary Cicero uses and that of Cato's definition discussed above. *Sermo* is the key word in both, standing for polite, informal conversation. The range through which speech must be effective is indicated in both cases by *circuli, convivia,* and *contiones.* Cato and Cicero may be drawing on the same source.

29. *Pro Sest.* 18.

30. *Pro Cael.* 33–36.

31. *Att.* 1.16.10; *In P. Clod. et C. Cur.*, frag. 22 (448, Schoell); also quoted by R. G. Austin in his edition of the *Pro Caelio*[3], 168. That the Roman was generally contemptuous of effeminacy in men may be seen from *Tusc.* 3.36. It is worth noting that the words *temperantia* and *modestia* have occurred in the sentence immediately preceding. Both are words that have been noted as prefacing a passage of the *De Officiis* which contains overtones of urbanity.

32. *Att.* 2.15.3.

33. *Carm.* 84.

34. There is enough evidence in Cicero's writings to show that correct use of the aspirate was expected of the urbanite, and that overuse of it was

considered an affectation. The evidence is gathered together in Ramage, "Note on Catullus' Arrius," *CP* 54 (1959), 44f.

35. Varro, *R.R.* 3.1.1 and 4f.

36. Cic., *De Har. Resp.* 56; *De Leg. Agr.* 2.79; *Part. Or.* 90.

37. Cf. Cic., *Phil.* 5.20 (*possessiones . . . et urbanas et rusticas*); *Qu. Fr.* 2.8.1 (*re . . . rustica, urbana*); *Qu. Fr.* 3.1.6 (*rebus rusticis* and *urbanam expolitionem*).

38. This is clearly implied by Cicero in *Pro Cael.* 54f. and by Sallust in *Orat. Macr. Trib. Pleb. ad Pleb.* 26f. (p. 161, Kurfess).

39. Cic., *Pro Rosc. Am.* 74f.

40. Cic., *De Off.* 1.130; *De Leg.* 1.6.

41. Cic., *Fam.* 5.12.1; *Pro Rosc. Am.* 20.

42. Cic., *Pro Quinct.* 59; *Pro Rosc. Am.* 143. Someone, probably a rustic, in Pomponius' *Aleones* says: *at ego rusticatim tangam*; *urbanatim nescio* (Nonius, p. 245 [Lindsay]). Cf. Cic., *De Div.* 1.55.

43. The use of *agrestis* and *rusticus* by Cicero shows that these characteristics included an insensitivity to the world around, an indifference to knowledge, a stubbornness, a coarseness of wit, a boldness and impetuosity, as well as a general lack of sophistication and any feelings of humanity. Cf. *Att.* 12.36.2 and 12.46.1; *Brut.* 286; *De Fin.* 3.37; *De Off.* 3.39; *De Or.* 2.10; *Fam.* 15.9.1 and 4; *Part. Or.* 92; *Post Red. in Sen.* 13f.; *Pro Arch.* 17; *Pro Planc.* 35; *Pro Sest.* 82.

44. *Pro Rosc. Am.* 44.

45. *Phil.* 8.9. In *De Off.* 1.129, Cicero-Panaetius says that one must avoid rusticity in his speech and general habits. The rough, unkempt countryman is in Catullus' mind as he tells Rufus that he smells bad (*Carm.* 69).

46. *De Fin.* 2.77; *Or.* 81.

47. *De Or.* 3.42–46.

48. The *concursus hiulcus* is mentioned in *De Or.* 3.171. See Wilkins' note on *hiulce* in his edition of the *De Oratore*, p. 433, and on the *concursus hiulcus*, p. 504.

49. The use of *rustice* here to define rustic speech is one of a number of indications that Cicero is encountering difficulties of analysis and definition.

50. *De Or.* 3.46. See also E. H. Sturtevant, *The Pronunciation of Greek and Latin*, 107–15, where the author treats the Latin vowels *e* and *i*. Toward the end of this discussion he singles out "a long vowel intermediate between *ē* and *ī*" (114) and suggests that it was this sound that Cicero was criticizing in Cotta's speech here in the *De Oratore*.

51. *R. R.* 1.2.14, 1.48.2.

52. *L. L.* 5.97.

53. Sturtevant (*Pronunciation*, 124–27) discusses this rustic pronunciation of *ae* at some length. Cotta's flat pronunciation is the subject for discussion again in the *Brutus* (259) where the drawing out of letters is called *subagreste* and *plane subrusticum*.

54. It is interesting to speculate on the possibility that Laberius' *Late Loquentes* may have been based on this characteristic of rustic speech.

55. Aul. Gell., *N. A.* 13.6.3: *rusticus fit sermo . . . si adspires perperam.* Sturtevant (*Pronunciation*, 131) points to another rustic-urban speech difference which Cicero does not mention. This is the appearance of a rustic *ō* for the urban *au*.

In *Or.* 161, Cicero says: *Quin etiam, quod iam subrusticum videtur, olim autem politius, eorum verborum, quorum eaedem erant postremae duae litterae, quae sunt in 'optimus,' postremam litteram detrahebant, nisi vocalis insequebatur.* Perhaps there is a hint here as to another characteristic of rustic speech. See also Eduard Mészáros, "Horatius rusticus," *Antik Tanulmányok* (*Studia Antiqua*) 2 (1955), 71–77. This work is summarized in *Bibliotheca Classica Orientalis* 2 (1957), cols. 85–92. In it the many instances of the *sermo vulgaris* in Horace's poetry are discussed at some length.

56. *Brut.* 137. A man such as Marius who was noted for his rusticity could get to the top at Rome (Cic., *In Pis.* 58; *Tusc.* 2.53). The reason for mention of his rusticity is perhaps the fact that it was unusual to find such a man in this position. Cf. Vell. Pat. 2.11.1.

57. *Att.* 9.13.4, 9.15.3; *Comm. Pet.* 31; *Pro Sest.* 97.

58. *De Leg.* 2.5.

59. *In P. Clod. et C. Cur.*, frag. 20 (447, Schoell); also quoted by R. G. Austin in his edition of the *Pro Caelio*[3], 166.

60. *Phil.* 3.15f.

61. *Att.* 2.11.2, 2.16.4.

62. *Fam.* 7.1.3.

63. *Brut.* 169–72.

64. Varro (*L. L.* 5.77) uses *vernaculus* in much the same sense when discussing the names of sea animals. Its opposite in this passage is *peregrinus.* Quintilian also mentions Tinca, although he seems to be dealing with less subtle failings than Cicero (*Inst. Orat.* 1.5.12).

65. *Brut.* 242: *oppidano quodam et incondito genere dicendi.*

66. *Brut.* 171.

67. *Comm. Pet.* 54.

68. *Fam.* 7.32.2: *urbanitatis possessionem, amabo, quibusvis interdictis defendamus; . . .*

69. *Fam.* 9.15.2.

70. *Qu. Fr.* 1.1.27; *Verr.* 2.5.150; *De Or.* 1.15.

71. *Pro Font.* 27.

72. *Comm. Pet.* 54.

73. *Brut.* 258. Cf. *Brut.* 51 where Cicero says that the Athenian eloquence, as soon as it left the Piraeus and went on its way through the islands of Asia, lost the health and vigor of Attic diction along with its purity.

74. *Brut.* 260. O. Jahn and Martha in their editions of the *Brutus* suggest this Greek original. Piderit (rev. by Friederich) believes that the Latin word is a translation of the Greek κατάπτυστα. That vocabulary is involved is also indicated by the fact that in other contexts *insolentia* is used applying mainly to a choice of words. E.g., *De Or.* 3.50.

75. *Pro Arch.* 26: *pingue quiddam sonantibus atque peregrinum.*

76. *De Leg.* 1.7; *Brut.* 228.

77. *Pro Font.* 11 f.

78. *Fam.* 9.15.2.

79. *Div. in Caec.* 39.

80. *Fam.* 7.31.2.

81. Theodore Mommsen, *The History of Rome* (Glencoe, Illinois, 1957), 5, 452 (rp.).

CHAPTER V
THE AUGUSTAN AGE

1. On Maecenas see Walter C. Summers, "On Some Fragments of Maecenas," *CQ* 2 (1908), 173. Whether Maecenas wrote a *De Cultu* or not depends on a reading in the letter of Seneca (114.4) in which he describes Maecenas' character. Summers (172) feels that ". . . the words 'Maecenas de cultu suo' are almost certainly interpolated . . ." and omits them in his *Select Letters of Seneca* (London, 1910), 139. L. D. Reynolds, in his recent edition, *L. Annaei Senecae ad Lucilium Epistulae Morales* (Oxford, 1965) (*OCT*), 2, 481, brackets these words and in a note *ad loc.* gives a history of scholarship on the text. On Agrippa see Pliny, *N. H.* 35.26.

2. Eduard Fraenkel, *Horace*, 399.

3. Walter Allen, Jr., "On the Friendship of Lucretius with Memmius," *CP* 33 (1938), 172.

4. Lammermann, *Von der attischen Urbanität*, 18.

5. Both Kiessling-Heinze and Wilkins in their editions of Horace's *Epistles* connect these two passages. See notes *ad loc.*

6. *Sat.* 1.2.25–28.

7. Cicero (*Brut.* 180) speaks of a Gargonius of Sulla's time as one of a group of orators *qui et plane indocti et inurbani aut rustici etiam fuerunt.*

8. *Sat.* 1.3.29–34.

9. *Ep.* 1.1.94–105.

10. Maenius in *Ep.* 1.15.26–32 has much in common with this prankster, and he too is apparently called urbane in an atmosphere of irony and sarcasm. It is tempting to connect *urbanus* and *scurra* very closely here as Kiessling-Heinze suggest in a note. They mention Plautus, *Trin.* 202, but strangely enough make no reference to *Most.* 15. In *Ep.* 1.19.15–18, Iarbitas is described as destroying himself while aiming at a reputation for urbane wit and eloquence by trying to imitate an inurbane Timagenes. If Iarbitas was a Moor, then he was compounding a felony, and it is easy to see how he failed.

11. *A.P.* 270–74.

12. *De Off.* 1.104. Fiske (*Lucilius and Horace,* 98) puts it this way: ". . . the contrast between *inurbanus* and *lepidus* clearly shows that the quality of *urbanitas* by which Horace and the Augustan age set so much store, is denied to the Plautine type of humor."

13. *Sat.* 1.4.7–13, 1.10.64–71.

14. *Odes* 1.18.9–11, 1.27.1–8, 1.36.10–16, 1.38, 2.6.1–12, 2.7.26f., 2.20.13–20.

15. *Odes* 3.1.41–48, 3.6.37–44, 4.5.29–36. H. Kier (*De laudibus vitae rusticae,* 108) points to the frequent reference to the Sabines in this kind of context.

16. Cf. the picture of peace, quiet, and sleep in the country in *Odes* 3.1.21–24 and the urban-rustic contrast in *Odes* 3.29.1–28.

17. R. Hirzel, *Der Dialog,* 2, 5.

18. *Ep.* 1.10.

19. There is another group that seems to fall somewhere between Horace and Aristius in its attitudes. Alfius in *Epode* 2 is always on the point of becoming a rustic, but cannot bring himself to give up his money-making. There is also the lawyer in *Sat.* 1.1.9–19 who would not change places with a countryman if he were given a chance to do so.

20. *Ep.* 1.7.73–95.

21. *Ep.* 1.2.41ff.

22. *Ep.* 1.12.11–15.

23. *Ep.* 2.2.38ff.

24. *Sat.* 2.2.2f.

25. *Sat.* 1.7.28–31.

26. *Ep.* 2.2.122–25.

27. *Ep.* 2.1.139–67.

28. *Ep.* 2.1.167. That he is talking about refinement or the lack of it

throughout this passage may be gathered from his use of *incultis versibus* in l.233. See Fraenkel, *Horace*, 392.

29. T. F. Higham, "Ovid: Some Aspects of His Character and Aims," *CR* 48 (1934), 113, n. 4.

30. *Ibid.*, 114.

31. L. P. Wilkinson, *Ovid Recalled*, 294.

32. *R. A.* 152; *Ex Pont.* 1.8.29; *Nux* 137.

33. *Fasti* 1.225.

34. Cf. *Fasti* 4.107 f. for a reference to the evolution of *cultus.*

35. *A. A.* 3.341 f. Cf. Lygdamus 1.17.

36. Brooks Otis, *Ovid as an Epic Poet*, 20.

37. T. F. Higham, "Ovid," *CR* 48 (1934), 114 f. Unfortunately, Higham goes on to generalize about Ovid's feeling for the countryside without considering all the evidence (116).

38. *A. A.* 3.133–68. Tibullus speaks of a *culta puella* as one with hair done up (1.9.67–72).

39. This may be gathered by inference from *R. A.* 335. But cf. *A. A.* 3.293–96 where it appears that the young lady may lisp slightly to give attractiveness to her speech. See T. F. Higham, "Ovid and Rhetoric," in *Ovidiana, recherches sur Ovide*, ed. by N. I. Herescu, 45.

40. *A. A.* 1.459–524. Ovid calls him *bene cultus.* This use recalls the *cultus* that the young woman is told to avoid at 3.433f.

41. Hermann Fränkel, *Ovid: A Poet Between Two Worlds*, 208, n. 7.

42. *Ibid.*, 70.

43. *R. A.* 247f.

44. *R. A.* 225f.

45. Fr. Lenz ("Ovid," *Jahresb.* 264 [1939], 53) and Fränkel (*Ovid*, 208, n. 7) both use this passage to show that Ovid has a positive feeling for the country.

46. Cf. *Tr.* 3.1, where there is a longing for and even a savoring of the city and all its parts. In *Ex Pont.* 3.1.11–28, the poet presents a similar picture of spring in the Italian countryside which is meant to serve as a contrast with life in Pontus.

47. *Ex Pont.* 1.8.41–60.

48. Ll. 29 f.: *nec tu credideris urbanae commoda vitae/quaerere Nasonem;* *quaerit et illa tamen.*

49. Ll. 39 f.: *at, puto, sic urbis misero est erepta voluptas,/quolibet ut saltem rure frui liceat!*

50. *Ep.* 2.1.146. In *Am.* 2.4.19 the same development may be implied in

the statement that Callimachus' poetry is considered by some to be rough and rustic (*rustica*) compared with Ovid's.

51. Propertius (2.19.13f.) suggests the roughness of the country in the shrine that is *incultus* and next to rustic hearths (*agrestes . . . focos*). He also uses *incultus* cleverly in 1.18.28.

52. *Am.* 1.8.43f.

53. *A. A.* 1.607f., 671ff. Cf. *A. A.* 2.565f.

54. *Am.* 3.4.37f.: *Rusticus est nimium, quem laedit adultera coniunx/et notos mores non satis urbis habet.*

55. There are other instances of the opposition between rusticity and love: *Am.* 3.1.43, 3.6.88; *Her.* 1.77f. Propertius (2.5.21–26) presents a picture of a roaring, wrangling, uncontrolled rustic lover.

56. The adjective *barbarus* appears in the *Ex Ponto* 11 times and in the *Tristia* 21 times.

57. He describes them as *inhumani* in *Ex Pont.* 1.5.66 and 3.5.28.

58. *Tr.* 3.8.37–40.

59. One of the best pictures of these people is in *Tr.* 5.7. See also *Tr.* 5.10.27–44; *Ex Pont.* 3.5.6, 4.2.2.

60. *Ex Pont.* 4.2.37f.; *Tr.* 3.14.35–46, 4.1.90–94.

61. *Tr.* 5.2.67f. and 5.7.51f. The situation was quite different here from that at Massilia in the early second century B.C. Cf. Livy, *Hist.* 37.54.18–24.

62. *Tr.* 5.12.55–58.

63. *Ex Pont.* 3.2.40, 4.13.17–24.

64. *Tr.* 5.1.69–74.

65. *Tr.* 3.1.17f., 3.14.46–50.

66. *Ex Pont.* 1.1.3; *Tr.* 1.1.3, 3.1.11–20.

67. *Tr.* 3.12.39–44, 4.1.87–94.

68. *Ex Pont.* 2.4.1–22.

69. A similar atmosphere pervades the letter to Maximus Cotta (*Ex Pont.* 3.5).

70. *Contr.* 9.4.17. Cf. *Suas.* 2.12 where Sabinus is called a *venustissimus . . . scurra.*

71. *Suas.* 7.13.

72. *Contr.* 9.4.19f.

73. There is much the same personal irony and sarcasm in Pacatus' jeering greeting to Moschus which is described by Seneca as *non inurbane* (*Contr.* 10. *praef.* 10). There is a similar use of *urbane* in *Contr.* 9.3.13.

74. *Inst. Orat.* 6.3.102–12. Most of what is said about the *De Urbanitate* in these pages is adapted from Ramage, "The *De Urbanitate* of Domitius Marsus," *CP* 54 (1959), 250–55.

75. *Inst. Orat.* 6.3.102.

76. See Ramage, "The *De Urbanitate* of Domitius Marsus," *CP* 54 (1959), 251 f. Quintilian spends some time discussing these in *Inst. Orat.* 8.5.1–34.

77. On the pointed style in general see Summers, *Select Letters of Seneca,* Introduction A ("The Pointed Style in Greek and Roman Literature"), xv–xli.

78. On the development of the literary epigram see C. W. Mendell, "Martial and the Satiric Epigram," *CP* 17 (1922), 1–20.

79. *Att.* 1.3. The words that describe his voice are *summa suavitas oris atque vocis.*

80. *Att.* 4.1.

81. *De Or.* 3.42f.

82. *Contr.* 3. *praef.* 3.

83. *Suas.* 2.16: *municipalis orator.*

84. *Contr.* 1. *praef.* 14ff.

85. *Contr.* 2.4.8: *Latini utique sermonis observator diligentissimus.*

86. *Suas.* 6.27.

87. *Inst. Orat.* 1.5.55f., 8.1.1ff.

88. K. Latte, "Livy's *Patavinitas,*" *CP* 35 (1940), 57, 59. G. L. Hendrickson ("A Witticism of Asinius Pollio," *AJP* 36 [1915], 74f.) apparently feels the same way. Müller (*Leben und Werke des Gaius Lucilius,* 24) says that Livy's *Patavinitas* was opposed to *urbanitas.*

89. J. Whatmough, "Quemadmodum Pollio reprehendit in Livio Patavinitatem?" *HSCP* 44 (1933), 97. Cf. 103f.

90. *Ibid.,* 105.

91. *Ibid.,* 116ff. He would make Catullus' Arrius who exhibited improper use of the aspirate a product of northern Italy.

92. *Inst. Orat.* 1.7.24.

93. *Inst. Orat.* 1.7.13.

94. Whatmough, "Quemadmodum Pollio reprehendit in Livio Patavinitatem?" *HSCP* 44 (1933), 99f. There is possibly more at work here as Lindsay suggests (*The Latin Language,* 424, 607).

95. R. Syme (*The Roman Revolution* [Oxford, 1939], 485f.) suggests that a broader criticism of Livy was involved in Pollio's remark. Cf. also Hendrickson, "A Witticism of Asinius Pollio," *AJP* 36 (1915), 71 and W. H. Alexander, "Patavinitas," *CW* 43 (1949), 245. There can be little doubt, however, that the criticism as it is treated by Quintilian applied only to matters of speech.

CHAPTER VI
THE FIRST CENTURY AFTER CHRIST

1. M. Rostovtzeff, *The Social and Economic History of the Roman Empire* (rev. by P. M. Fraser), I, 103.
2. *De Cons.* 6.2–6.
3. Val. Max. 9.12. *ext.* 6. Columella, R. R. 8.16.3. Petr., *Sat.* 48.
4. Petr., *Sat.* 39.
5. 6.2. *ext.* 2: *urbana libertas, faceta audacia.* Another instance in the *Satyricon* (116) confirms this connection between the adjective and a lack of restraint.
6. Sen., *Tr. Anim.* 6.2.
7. Sen., *Const. Sap.* 17.3. Cf. *De Ira* 2.23.5.
8. Sen., *De Ira* 3.23.4: *temeraria urbanitas*; *Const. Sap.* 11.3: *urbanitas . . . contumeliosa.* The same thing is referred to a little later (17.2) when Seneca speaks of those who are *petulantibus et per contumeliam urbanis.* Eumolpus' *dicta* in the *Satyricon* (109) make up a very dull show of wit: *frigidissima urbanitate.*
9. Petr., *Sat. 36, 52.*
10. Val. Max. 7.5.2: *contumeliosam urbanitatem.*
11. An interesting extension in meaning occurs when Pliny the Elder, as he writes about trees in his *Natural History* (16.78), notes two kinds, the *silvestres* and the *urbani.* The former are those which grow wild without man's help, while the latter are the class of "cultivated" (*mites*) trees which provide fruit and shade and are, as a rule, of the most value to humans. The use of *urbanus* here is very interesting, for from the refinement and cultivation of city life it has come to be applied to agricultural "cultivation." There are perhaps two levels of meaning in the word: it seems to signify something that contributes to the ease and refinement of the city-dweller, but at the same time describes something that has undergone cultivation.
12. *Ep.* 51.10. This is part of a more general criticism of the city for the debilitating effect that it has on people living there. Cf. Col., *R. R.* 1.8.1 and Celsus, *De Med.* 1.2.1.
13. *De Ira* 1.18.2.
14. *Ep.* 114.12.
15. This is implied in Phaedrus' fable of the *scurra* and *rusticus* (5.5).
16. The latter adjective recalls the passage in Pliny the Elder discussed above (note 11) in which the *arbores urbaniores* are also described as *mites.*
17. R. R. 1. *praef.* 7–17, 8.16.2, 12.46.1.
18. *Ep.* 90.19.

19. *Ep.* 86.11. Surely a similar attitude is implied in Seneca's statement (*Ep.* 122.6) that the youth of his time thinks it is countryfied to drink after dinner rather than before. Cf. *De Ben.* 1.9.3 where *rusticus* is used in much the same way as Ovid uses it to refer to the man who does not understand modern habits.

20. Sen., *De Ben.* 2.3.2.

21. Sen., *Nat. Quaest.* 4. *praef.* 5. Cf. Calpurnius, *Ecl.* 4.14 where *rusticitas* is an uncouthness and lack of polish in song and verse.

22. Sen., *De Ben.* 1.11.6.

23. Col., *R. R.* 9.14.12: *pinguioribus . . . rusticorum litteris.*

24. Phaedr., 4.25.10; Sen., *Apoc.* 2.

25. *Ep.* 15.8.

26. There is nothing else on the subject of rustic speech except for a few references to vocabulary. Cf. Pliny, *N. H.* 1. *praef.* 12f. and Columella, *R. R.* 3.13.11, 5.1.5, 5.5.16, 8.5.4.

27. *Ecl.* 7.

28. *De Ira* 3.18.1.

29. *Ecl.* 2.61.

30. *De Cons.* 18.9.

31. *Dial.* 9: *conversatio amicorum et iucunditas urbis.*

32. Tac., *Dial.* 7.

33. Esp. *Sat.* 3.34–37, 60–65.

34. Tac., *Hist.* 2.21.

35. Tac., *Hist.* 2.88.

36. Further insight into the thinking of Vitellius' soldiers is to be gained from *Hist.* 2.74. In spite of their rough appearance and uncouth way of speaking, they insist on looking down on others. This is surely an example of the *provincialium superbia* which Tacitus mentions in the *Annals* (15.20f.).

37. 10.58.6, 12.57.

38. 10.12. At 1.55.13f. Martial wishes this pallor on the man who does not like him and his country life.

39. Grundy Steiner, "Columella and Martial on Living in the Country," *CJ* 50 (1954), 88f. In 4.64 Martial strikes a new note when he lashes out at the unproductive villa situated on the edge of the city. Cf. 3.47 and 12.72.

40. Cf. 4.55 where Spanish names come tripping off his tongue followed by a brief but emphatic defense of his mention of them.

41. 1.41. There is an interesting reference to Gabba, the court jester, once again in 10.101 where Capitolinus is described as being so humorous that

Gabba becomes *rusticus*. The implication is strong here and in the passage above that Gabba had a reputation for *urbanitas* in wit. One wonders also if Caecilius and Valens did not have much in common when it came to wit. Tacitus says (*Hist.* 3.62) that Valens sought a reputation for *urbanitas per lasciviam*.

42. 3.63. Cf. 3.55 and 2.12.

43. 3.24. *Rusticus* is still used as an adjective of depreciation as in 14.46.

44. *Spect.* 3.

45. Quintilian's words are *color dicendi* and *orationis color*, while Cicero speaks of a *quadam quasi colorata oratio*. Quintilian also speaks of an ἀττικισμός *ille reddens Athenarum proprium saporem* which sounds like a combination of Cicero's *sapor vernaculus* and *Atticorum sonus*.

46. Perhaps now it is possible to see more clearly the point of Quintilian's reference to Marsus' mention of a *narrandi urbanitas* (6.3.105), for the teacher is in essence saying that, while Marsus saw what *urbanitas* really was, he concentrated on a minor aspect of it when he applied the word to epigram. The same feeling lies behind what he says about an *oratoria urbanitas*, which he places opposite displays of wit at banquets and in informal conversation (6.3.14), the latter being, presumably, what Cato was defining. It is easier to understand his purpose in dwelling on Cicero's observation that wit (*facetias*) exists in narration (*in narrando*), while *dicacitas* is related to attack (*iaciendo*) and takes the form of refined humor briefly and pointedly expressed (6.3.42ff.: *inclusa breviter urbanitas*). In each case, the author pits his concept of wit involving the whole flavor of speech against the idea of wit as epigrammatic expression. For a perceptive analysis of the kind of wit implied in *facetum* see 6.3.19f. where Quintilian dissociates it from *ridicula* and relates it to *decor* and *elegantia*. Cf. also 6.3.3f.

47. The city-country contrast is still recognized. In fact, a favorite topic for debate was whether city or country life was preferable (*Inst. Orat.* 2.4.24).

48. 2.5.8. At 6.3.14 Quintilian complains of the lack of exercises and teachers to promote this wit. The difficulties of dealing with this abstract feeling may in part account for this lack, and Quintilian attempts to remedy the situation in this long section by offering definition and description of cultured wit.

49. 6.3.26. He has more to say along these lines in 6.3.29f. and 6.1.46–49. Here there is an emphasis on good taste in gestures and facial expression, careful and not too frequent use of wit, and avoidance of the ridiculous.

50. 8.6.73f. In 6.3.8 *urbanitas* and *stultitia* are opposed once again.

51. 4.2.19. The anecdote is from *Pro Cluent.* 57f.

52. 6.3.81. Probably Quintilian is thinking of one or all of these when he speaks of "an urbane wit concisely expressed" at 6.3.43. That this wit can consist of one word is clear from his reference to Afer's use of *satagere* at 6.3.54. Cf. 11.3.126.

53. Another ironically urbane bit of wit of Cicero is recounted at 8.3.54.

54. 6.3.10. This story of Pyrrhus had been recounted by Valerius Maximus earlier (5.1. *ext.* 3). Cf. 6.3.98 where drawing upon history for a jest (*urbanitas*) is considered very learned.

55. On this see 1.5.3, 1.5.55, 1.5.57, 1.5.58.

56. *Resono* and *tinnitas* are so close to *resono* and *retinnio* in the *Brutus* (171) as to suggest that Quintilian may have had this passage in mind as he wrote.

57. 6. *praef.* 11. The terms he uses are *vocis iucunditas claritasque* and *oris suavitas.*

58. 1.11.4–7. The use of *pinguitudine* here recalls Cicero's criticism of the poets of Corduba in *Pro Arch.* 26.

59. Here may be the reason for Quintilian's not using *urbanitas* for a general culture. Perfect education leads to perfect oratory, and the ability to express oneself eloquently results in a refinement. Since he is dealing here with the attainment of eloquence through learning, it is only natural that he should use concrete terms from these two areas rather than less rigidly defined terms such as *urbanus* and *urbanitas.*

60. 7.9.13, 8.6.3.

61. See note 11.

62. Such balances must not be pressed too closely, however. Cf. *severitatem comitatemque* in 8.21.1.

63. 2.13.6: *Mira in sermone, mira etiam in ore ipso vultuque suavitas.* In another letter (5.5.1) Fannius is described as a *homo elegans disertus* where it is perhaps possible to see the close relationship between sophistication and eloquence.

64. 6.21.5, 9.22.2.

65. 5.20.6. The qualifiers are *callide, acriter,* and *culte.*

66. On these contrasting attitudes see A. N. Sherwin-White, *The Letters of Pliny* (Oxford, 1966), notes *ad* 5.14.8 (pp. 345f.), and 9.15.3 (p. 500).

67. In 9.15 Pliny writes in a strikingly similar way to Falco, complaining of the petitions of the rustics and their complaints that he must listen to, no matter how unwilling he may be.

68. 9.20.2. There is a similar feeling in 2.11.25 where he asks Arrianus to tell him about the *res rusticae* of his estate.

69. A. C. Andrews, "Pliny the Younger, Conformist," *CJ* 34 (1938), 154.

EPILOGUE

1. *N. A.* 12.12.1.
2. *N. A.* 15.5.3.
3. *Met.* 2.20: *lepidi sermonis . . . comitate.*
4. In *De Platone* 2.14 (239) Apuleius uses *urbanus* and *facetus* together to describe the souls that strive after the good. These seem to be almost divine and thoroughly uncorrupted, and they are searching for virtue.
5. Cf. *M. Caes.* 1.4, 3.20, 4.4. *Ant.* 2.3 (ed. by Naber).
6. Naber, 211–14, 214ff.
7. 10.3.14f.: *agresti aure.*
8. 13.21.7: *aure agresti.*
9. *M. Caes.* 3.15 (ed. by Naber): *At ego sine istis artibus omnem orationem absurdam et agrestem et incognitam, denique inertem atque inutilem puto.* C. R. Haines (*The Correspondence of Marcus Cornelius Fronto* [London, 1919–20] [*LCL*], 1, 100, n. 2) suggests that Fronto may have Quintilian's definition of *urbanitas* in mind here (*Inst. Orat.* 6.3.107).
10. *M. Ant. De Eloqu.* 3 (ed. by Naber). Haines (*The Correspondence of Fronto*, 2, 72) reads *lenis*; Naber reads [*amabilis*].
11. Ael. Spart., *Hadr.* 3.1.
12. Ael. Lamprid. (*Com.* 17.3) mentions that Commodus had a *sermo inconditus.* This appears to involve an unsophisticated roughness.
13. *Gall. Duo* 14.4: *urbanissime et prudentissime.* David Magie's translation (*The Scriptores Historiae Augustae* [London, 1932] [*LCL*], 3, 47), "with the greatest shrewdness and wisdom," seems to miss the point. De Saumaise in his note on this passage (I. Casaubon, Cl. de Saumaise, I. Gruter, *Historiae Augustae Scriptores VI* [Leyden, 1671], 2, 225) equates *urbane* with *comiter* and *benigne*, which is surely better. Is it possible that the combination has a Stoic connotation? See Appendix II. The same general connotation is probably to be read into *urbane* as Aelius Lampridius uses it in *Com.* 4.5.
14. *Prob.* 16.5: *vel per terrorem vel urbanitatem.* Magie's translation (*Scriptores Historiae Augustae*, 3, 369) is about as vague as the Latin and so begs the issue. De Saumaise (*Historiae Augustae Scriptores VI*, 2, 667), though he would rather read *per voluntatem* than *per urbanitatem*, does go on to relate this to Pollio's use of *urbanissime* and equates it with *courtoisie.*
15. Ael. Lamprid., *Alex. Sev.* 63.2.
16. Jul. Capit., *Maxim. Duo* 2.2, 2.5, 3.3.
17. Jul. Capit., *Clod. Alb.* 10.6.
18. Ael. Spart., *Sev.* 19.9: *canorus voce, sed Afrum quiddam usque ad senectutem sonans.*

19. *Praef. Hieron. In Lib. Is., Patrologia Latina* 28, 825. In one of his *Epistles* (57.12), Jerome expresses a preference for a *sancta simplicitas* over a *verbosa rusticitas.*

20. St. Augustine at one point in his *Confessions* (3.1) relates *urbanus* to vanity: . . . *et tamen foedus atque inhonestus, elegans et urbanus esse gestiebam abundanti vanitate.*

21. *Mor.* 10.360 (*Patrologia Latina* 75, 947).

22. St. Bonaventure, *Commentaria in Quatuor Libros Sententiarum* (Quaracchi, 1885), 2, 943.

23. John Stow, *A Survay of London* (ed. by C. L. Kingsford), 2, 196 f.

APPENDIX I
GREEK URBANITY TO THE FIFTH CENTURY B.C.

1. Cf. *Il.* 17.144 and the editions of van Leeuwen, Leaf, and Ameis-Hentze, notes *ad loc.* Perhaps, then, it is not technically correct to speak of the city in these times. But for the sake of simplicity, the term will be used to denote the major settlement of Homeric times which eventually developed into the full fledged city state.

2. *The City in History*, 134.

3. Cf. W. Warde Fowler's description of the city state and its institutions at this time in his *The City State of the Greeks and Romans*, 65–68.

4. *Od.* 1.185, 16.383, 24.212, 24.308. Ameis-Hentze, *Homers Odyssee*[10], Leipzig, 1895, commenting on the first passage, says: "ἐπ' ἀγροῦ: *auf dem Lande im Gegensatz zur Stadt.*" In Ameis-Hentze-Cauer, *Homers Odyssee*[13] (Leipzig, 1920), n. *ad loc.*, the observation has been changed: "*auf dem Lande, in der Feldmark.*"

5. *Il.* 23.832 and Leaf's edition, n. *ad loc.*

6. *Il.* 18.541–606. Cf. *The Shield of Heracles*, 270–304 which presents a similar description of town and country and which is perhaps patterned on this passage in the *Iliad.*

7. It is difficult to agree with Werner Jaeger (*Paideia: The Ideals of Greek Culture* [tr. by G. Highet], 1, 57) that in the time of Hesiod the rustic had not yet become associated with a lack of culture.

8. W. B. Stanford, *The Odyssey of Homer* (London, 1948), 2, 360, n. *ad loc.*

9. Ribbeck, *Agroikos*, 4. See also Jaeger's brief but clear treatment of this refinement (*Paideia*, 1, 19 f.).

10. Bergk 10 (2, p. 13). Cf. line 3 where city and fields are contrasted. Jaeger (*Paideia*, 1, 93) mentions the fact that Callinus and Tyrtaeus imitate the Homeric style, but show a new "sense of communal life."

11. *LG 27* (1, p. 336).
12. *LG 28* (1, p. 338).
13. *LG* 41.10 (1, p. 346); Bergk 23 (3, p. 156); Lobel-Page 112.10 (p. 158).
Cf. 426 (p. 286).
14. Jaeger, *Paideia*, 1, 197 f.
15. Bergk ll.53–58 (2, p. 124).
16. Bergk 3 (2, pp. 113 f.).
17. *LG 20* (2, p. 148); Bergk 130 (3, pp. 288 f.). Cf. *LG 76*. 7–11 (2, p. 176) and Bergk 63. 7–11 (3, p. 272).
18. *LG 97* (2, pp. 186 and 188). Max Treu (*Von Homer zur Lyrik*: *Wandlungen des griechischen Weltbildes im Spiegel der Sprache*² [Munich, 1968], 289ff.) points to Anacreon as an aristocrat who writes not of heroism, but of wine and love, and associates with men of urbane outlook.
19. *LG 2A* (1, p. 58); Bergk 24 (3, pp. 45 f.). There are textual problems throughout this fragment. For the sake of simplicity I have used Edmonds' text. If his reading ἄγροικος in the first line is correct, it represents the first occurrence of the word in Greek literature.
20. *LG 98* (1, p. 254); Bergk 70 (3, p. 112); Lobel-Page 57 (p. 40). Once again there are textual problems that are best avoided here. Athenaeus, *Deipn.* 1.21b, says that Andromeda is under criticism here. Cf. Denys Page, *Sappho and Alcaeus: An Introduction to the Study of Ancient Lesbian Poetry*, 133.
21. Ribbeck, *Agroikos*, 34.
22. Another fragment of Sappho (Lobel-Page 158 [p. 98]) in which Sappho says that a person should keep his tongue quiet in times of anger suggests another quality of this refinement. Cf. Plutarch, *De Cohib. Ira* 456 D–E.
23. Lobel-Page 130.15–20 (p. 178).
24. Cf. the fragment of Anacreon's *Hymn to Artemis* (Bergk 1.7 f. [3, p. 254]): οὐ γὰρ ἀνημέρους ποιμαίνεις πολιήτας. According to Edmonds the city is probably Ionian Magnesia (*LG*, 2, 137, n. 4).
25. Bergk 12 (2, p. 71): πολλὰ μέσοισιν ἄριστα· μέσος θέλω νὲν πόλει εἶναι.
26. Bergk 67 (3, p. 418).

APPENDIX II
THE STOIC *Urbanitas*

1. *Fam.* 3.7.5.
2. *Von der attischen Urbanität*, 24 f.
3. "Die *Urbanitas* nach Cicero" in *Festgabe für Wilhelm Crecelius*, 93.
4. R. Y. Tyrrell and L. C. Purser, *The Correspondence of M. Tullius*

Cicero[2] (Dublin, 1914), 3, 171, n. *ad loc.* They also point to a passage of Plutarch's *De Virtute Morali* (441B) in which the writer mentions such a plethora of virtues and includes εὐτραπελία among them.

5. Alain Michel (*Rhétorique et philosophie chez Cicéron*, 31) also equates *comitas* and *urbanitas.*

6. Cf. *De Fin.* 5.65: *iustitia . . . cui sunt adiunctae pietas, bonitas, liberalitas, benignitas, comitas quaeque sunt generis eiusdem.* Otto Heine (*M. Tullii Ciceronis De Officiis*[6] [Berlin, 1885], n. *ad* 3.24 [p. 183]) suggests that *comitas, iustitia,* and *liberalitas* are virtues which combine to produce the cardinal virtue *communitas.* The parallel he draws from the *De Officiis* (3.118) makes this seem highly likely.

BIBLIOGRAPHY

There has been very little written about Roman urbanity *per se*, although it often comes into discussions of Roman life and literature. The following list includes both those writings that treat the subject itself and those which deal with it incidentally. The works which treat some aspect of *urbanitas* directly and in detail are indicated by an asterisk (*). The more general social, economic, and literary histories have been omitted, though Tarn and Rostovtzeff appear simply because they have been so useful. Modern editions of the classical authors have also been omitted; those that contain useful exegesis may be found at the appropriate places in the Notes.

Alexander, W. H. "Patavinitas," *CW* 43 (1949/50), 245.

Allen, Walter, Jr. "On the Friendship of Lucretius with Memmius," *CP* 33 (1938), 167–81.

Andrews, A. C. "Pliny the Younger, Conformist," *CJ* 34 (1938/39), 143–54.

Beare, W. "Plautus and His Public," *CR* 42 (1928), 106–11.

Bergk, Th. *Kleine philologische Schriften*, ed. by R. Peppmüller. 2 vols. Halle, 1884–86.

*Bléry, H. *Rusticité et urbanité romaines*. Paris. 1909.

Brock, M. D. *Studies in Fronto and His Age*. Cambridge, 1911.

Brown, Ruth Martin. *A Study of the Scipionic Circle* (*Iowa Studies in Classical Philology* 1). Scottdale (Pa.), 1934.

Budinszky, A. *Die Ausbreitung der lateinischen Sprache über*

Italien und die Provinzen des römischen Reiches. Berlin, 1881.

Burke, Thomas. *The English Townsman²*. London, 1947.

Chalmers, W. R. "Plautus and His Audience" in *Roman Drama,* ed. by T. A. Dorey and Donald R. Dudley. New York, 1965, pp. 21–50.

Cichorius, Conrad. *Untersuchungen zu Lucilius.* Berlin, 1908.

D'Alton, John F. *Roman Literary Theory and Criticism.* New York, 1931.

De Graff, Thelma B. *Naevian Studies.* Geneva (N.Y.), 1931.

Dunham, F. S. "The Younger Pliny—Gentleman and Citizen," *CJ* 40 (1944/45), 417–26.

*Egermann, F. Review of Karl Lammermann, *Von der attischen Urbanität und ihrer Auswirkung in der Sprache, Gnomon* 13 (1937), 642–45.

Fiske, George C. "The Plain Style in the Scipionic Circle" in *University of Wisconsin Studies in Language and Literature* 3. Madison, 1919, pp. 62–105.

———. *Lucilius and Horace, A Study in the Classical Theory of Imitation (University of Wisconsin Studies in Language and Literature* 7). Madison, 1920.

Flickinger, Roy C. "Terence and Menander," *CJ* 26 (1930/31), 676–94.

Fowler, W. Warde. *The City State of the Greeks and Romans.* London, 1893 (rp. 1952).

Fraenkel, Eduard. *Plautinisches im Plautus.* Berlin, 1922.

———. *Horace.* Oxford, 1957 (paperbound 1966).

Fränkel, Hermann F. *Ovid: A Poet Between Two Worlds (Sather Classical Lectures* 18). Berkeley, 1945.

*Frank, Eva. *De vocis* urbanitas *apud Ciceronem vi atque usudiss.* Essen, 1932.

Giagrande, Giuseppe. "On the Origins of the Greek Romance: The Birth of a Literary Form," *Eranos* 60 (1962), 132–59.

Glover, T. R. *Virgil²*. New York, 1912.

Grassi, E. "Nota a Lucilio," *Atene e Roma,* n.s., 6 (1961), 148.

Grimal, Pierre. *Le siècle des Scipions*. Paris, 1953.

Grube, G. M. A. *A Greek Critic: Demetrius on Style (Phoenix Supplement 4)*. Toronto, 1961.

Gugel, H. "Die Urbanität im Rednerdialog des Tacitus," *Symbolae Osloenses* 42 (1967), 127–40.

Hadas, Moses. *Three Greek Romances*. Garden City, N. Y., 1953.

Haffter, Heinz. "Terenz und seine künstlerische Eigenart," *Museum Helveticum* 10 (1953), 1–20, 73–102.

*Heerdegen, Ferdinand. *De vocabuli quod est urbanus apud vetustiores scriptores Latinos vi atque usu*. Erlangen, 1918.

Heitland, W. E. *Agricola, A Study of Agriculture and Rustic Life in the Greco-Roman World from the Point of View of Labour*. Cambridge, 1921.

*Henderson, Charles, Jr. "A Lexicon of the Stylistic Terms Used in Roman Literary Criticism" (unpublished diss.). Chapel Hill, 1955.

Hendrickson, G. L. "A Witticism of Asinius Pollio," *AJP* 36 (1915), 70–75.

———. "Horace and Valerius Cato II," *CP* 12 (1917), 77–92.

Higham, T. F. "Ovid: Some Aspects of His Character and Aims," *CR* 48 (1934), 105–16.

———. "Ovid and Rhetoric" in *Ovidiana, recherches sur Ovide*, ed. by N. I. Herescu. Paris, 1958, pp. 32–48.

Hirzel, Rudolf. *Der Dialog*. 2 vols. Leipzig, 1895.

Jaeger, Werner. *Paideia: The Ideals of Greek Culture*, tr. by Gilbert Highet. 3 vols. Oxford, 1943–60.

Jones, A. H. M. "The Social Structure of Athens in the Fourth Century B.C.," *Economic History Review* 2 ser., 8 (1955/56), 141–55.

Jüthner, J. *Hellenen und Barbaren*. Leipzig, 1923.

———. "Isokrates und die Menschheitsidee," *Wiener Studien* 47 (1929), 26–31.

Kier, Hermann. *De laudibus vitae rusticae* (diss.). Marburg, 1933.

Knoche, Ulrich. "Über die Aneignung griechischer Poesie im älteren Rom," *Gymnasium* 65 (1958), 321–40.

Korfmacher, William. "'Grecizing' in Lucilian Satire," *CJ* 30 (1934/35), 453–62.

Krauss, F. B. "The Motive of Martial's Satire," *CW* 38 (1944/45), 18–20.

*Lammermann, Karl. *Von der attischen Urbanität und ihrer Auswirkung in der Sprache* (diss.). Göttingen, 1935.

Latte, Kurt. "Livy's *Patavinitas,*" *CP* 35(1940), 56–60.

Lenz, Fr. "Ovid." Bericht über das Schrifttum der Jahre 1928–1937, *Jahresb.* 264 (1939), 1–168.

Leo, F. "Die römische Poesie in der sullanischen Zeit," *Hermes* 49 (1914), 161–95.

*Lutsch, Otto. "Die *Urbanitas* nach Cicero" in *Festgabe für Wilhelm Crecelius.* Elberfeld, 1881, pp. 80–95.

Manzo, A. *Facete Dicta Tulliana.* Turin, 1969.

Marmorale, Enzo V. *Naevius Poeta*[2]. Florence, 1950.

Marouzeau, Jules. "Notes sur la fixation du Latin classique," *Mémoires de la Société Linguistique de Paris* 17 (1911), 266–80.

———. "Plaute et la première 'crise du Latin'," *REL* 4 (1926), 99–103.

Mendell, C. W. "Martial and the Satiric Epigram," *CP* 17 (1922), 1–20.

Mészáros, Eduard. "Horatius rusticus," *Antik Tanulmányok* (*Studia Antiqua*) 2 (1955), 71–77. Summary in *Bibliotheca Classica Orientalis* 2 (1957), cols. 85–92.

Michel, Alain. *Rhétorique et philosophie chez Cicéron.* Paris, 1960.

Müller, L. *Leben und Werke des Gaius Lucilius.* Leipzig, 1876.

Mumford, Lewis. *The City in History.* New York, 1961.

Munk, Eduard. *De Fabulis Atellanis.* Leipzig, 1840.

Otis, Brooks. *Ovid as an Epic Poet*[2]. Cambridge, 1970.

Page, Denys L. *Sappho and Alcaeus: An Introduction to the Study of Ancient Lesbian Poetry.* Oxford, 1955.

Palmer, L. R. *The Latin Language.* London, 1954.

Perry, Ben Edwin. *The Ancient Romances: A Literary-Historical*

Account of Their Origins (Sather Classical Lectures 37). Berkeley, 1967.

Phillimore, J. S. "The Greek Romances," in *English Literature and the Classics*, ed. by G. S. Gordon, Oxford, 1912, pp. 87–117.

*Ramage, E. S. "Note on Catullus' Arrius," *CP* 54 (1959), 44 f.

*———. "The *De Urbanitate* of Domitius Marsus," *CP* 54 (1959), 250–55.

*———. "Early Roman Urbanity," *AJP* 81 (1960), 65–72.

*———. "Cicero on Extra-Roman Speech," *TAPA* 92 (1961), 481–94.

*———. "*Urbanitas:* Cicero and Quintilian, a Contrast in Attitudes," *AJP* 84 (1963), 390–414.

———. "City and Country in Menander's *Dyskolos,*" *Philologus* 110. (1966), 194–211.

Rattenbury, R. M. "Romance: Trails of Lost Greek Novels" in *New Chapters in the History of Greek Literature* 3 ser., ed. by J. U. Powell. Oxford, 1933, pp. 211–57.

Renard, M. "La 'Cistellaria' de Plaute et les menées étrusques en faveur de Carthage," *Latomus* 2 (1938), 77–83.

*Ribbeck, Otto. *Agroikos, eine ethologische Studie* in *Abhandlungen der philologisch—historischen Klasse der königlich sächsischen Gesellschaft der Wissenschaften* 10 (1888), pp. 1–68.

Rieth, Otto. *Die Kunst Menanders in den "Adelphen" des Terenz.* Hildesheim, 1964.

Ripert, Émile. *Ovide, poète de l'amour, des dieux et de l'exil.* Paris, 1921.

Roberts, W. Rhys. *The Ancient Boeotians: Their Character and Culture, and Their Reputation.* Cambridge, 1895.

Rohde, Erwin. *Der griechische Roman und seine Vorläufer*[4]. Hildesheim, 1960.

Rostovtzeff, M. *The Social and Economic History of the Hellenistic World.* 3 vols. Oxford, 1941.

———. *The Social and Economic History of the Roman Empire*[2], rev. by P. M. Fraser. 2 vols. Oxford, 1957.

*Saint-Denis, E. de. "Évolution sémantique de 'urbanus-urbanitas,'" *Latomus* 3 (1939), 5–24.

———. *Essais sur le rire et le sourire des Latins* (Publications de l'université de Dijon 32). Paris, 1965.

Schulten, A. *Sertorius.* Leipzig, 1926.

Shero, L. R. "Lucilius's *Cena Rustica,*" *AJP* 50 (1929), 64–70.

Skutsch, O. "Enniana V," *CQ* 57 (1963), 89–100.

Steiner, Grundy. "Columella and Martial on Living in the Country," *CJ* 50 (1954/55), 85–90.

Stow, John. *A Survay of London. Conteyning the Originall, Antiquity, Increase, Moderne estate, and description of that City,* ed. by Charles L. Kingsford. 2 vols. Oxford, 1908.

Straaten, Modestus van. *Panétius, sa vie, ses écrits et sa doctrine avec une édition des fragments.* Amsterdam, 1946.

Sturtevant, E. H. *The Pronunciation of Greek and Latin. The Sounds and Accents*². Philadelphia, 1940.

Summers, Walter C. "On Some Fragments of Maecenas," *CQ* 2 (1908), 170–74.

Tarn, W. W. *Hellenistic Civilization*³, rev. by G. T. Griffith. London, 1952.

Todd, F. A. *Some Ancient Novels.* London, 1940.

Toliver, Hazel M. "The Terentian Doctrine of Education," *CW* 43 (1949/50), 195–200.

Ullman, B. L. "Satura and Satire," *CP* 8 (1913), 172–94.

———. "The Present Status of the *Satura* Question," *Studies in Philology* 17 (1920), 379–401.

Veblen, Thorstein. *The Theory of the Leisure Class.* New York, 1912.

Waszink, J. H. "Tradition and Personal Achievement in Early Latin Literature," *Mnemosyne* 13, 4 ser., (1960), 16–33.

Webster, T. B. L. *Studies in Menander*². Manchester, 1960.

*Whatmough, Joshua. "Quemadmodum Pollio reprehendit in Livio Patavinitatem?" *HSCP* 44 (1933), 95–130.

Wilkinson, L. P. *Ovid Recalled.* Cambridge, 1955.

INDICES

I. INDEX OF WORDS
AND PHRASES

II. INDEX OF PASSAGES CITED

III. GENERAL INDEX